IN SEARCH OF
HOLY RUSSIA

IN SEARCH OF HOLY RUSSIA

FATHER SPYRIDON BAILEY

Published in 2020 by FeedARead.com Publishing
Financed by The Arts Council of Great Britain

A CIP catalogue record for this title is available from
the British Library.

Cover photograph by Father Spyridon
Back cover portrait by the artist Svetlana Solo-Orlova

To Svetlana,
thank you for your enthusiasm and for connecting
me with so many people in Russia.

Chapter One

The news that I was planning to visit Moscow was met with a mixed response. Those in my church community began to ask where I was visiting, and Russian friends excitedly recommended churches and monasteries. But others warned me to be careful, they expressed concern over some unnamed threat that they believed existed in Russia. The impact of continuous, negative stories coming from the news media had created a strange sense of danger that they thought I was going to be exposed to. It was enough to lead me to search out information on the internet about gangsters pretending to be taxi drivers who would drive unsuspecting tourists out to deserted places where they would threaten violence and demand money. This particular detail stayed with me for the whole trip and I was to eye taxis driving by with a great deal of suspicion.

In January 2020 I retired from teaching. My wife had always wanted to visit Moscow, and when I talked about making a pilgrimage to one or more monasteries she immediately suggested the destination. Without a hint of concern to fulfil her own ambitions, she insisted I make the journey alone. The plan took root and within the week I had written to my bishop for a blessing to make the trip. Confident in his response I searched for monasteries that were within the immediate vicinity of Moscow because I was wary of using Russian public transport. I was surprised at how many monasteries were in or around the capital, and I began sending emails asking if I could stay for a day or two. My hope was to find enough that would fill an eight day trip.

The bishop gave his blessing and supplied a letter of introduction that confirmed my identity as a priest. This document gave me a lot of confidence, I felt sure it would be enough to overcome any difficulties I might face. Russia demands that, with the exception of a few countries, foreign visitors must apply for a visa in order to enter. More research on the internet informed me that this could be a slow and complicated process, and that some people were turned down because they had made simple mistakes on their application form. Discussing this with one of my Russian friends she assured me that it wouldn't be a problem, and provided me with a company that would assist in the process. A quick glance at the visa application form made me realise I wouldn't be able to fill it in without assistance: it insisted on an official tourist voucher that was issued from Russia as well as the addresses of the places where I would be staying. Since I hadn't heard back from any of the monasteries I was unsure what to do, but my friend encouraged me to put myself in the hands of the company she was recommending. The cost of their service was twenty five pounds, which was cheaper than many I had seen advertising the same help, and it turned out to be money well spent. I filled in the application form as best I could. It included questions about where my parents had died, my employment record, and the dates of every trip I had made abroad in the last ten years. It also warned that any passport that had a creased or marked cover would result in a rejected application. There were a lot of unanswered questions on the form when I sent it to the company for review, but to my surprise it returned not only with a completed tourist voucher, but with all of the sections now completed. It now had a full schedule of hotels that I was to claim I was staying at, and it was suggested that I change some of my answers to increase the likelihood of my visa being issued. As this was the first time I had applied for a visa for any country, I was a little nervous about following their advice, but did as I was told.

In order to apply for the visa, travellers must visit one of three visa centres located in London, Manchester or Edinburgh. No appointments are offered, it is a case of first come first served. Someone told me they had spent a whole day waiting to be seen at the centre in London, so I chose Manchester and set off to arrive before nine in the morning. It was now late January, and Manchester was wet and grey as I found a multi-storey car park which I hoped wasn't too far from my destination. As I descend the concrete stairs I had to step over empty beer cans and used syringes, and there was evidence that a number of people had been sleeping there. The graffiti covering the walls created an atmosphere of threat, and I was relieved to step out into the busy street below. The majority of people milling around were Asian, most of the women wore Muslim head coverings of one kind or another, and dressed in my rassa with a pectoral cross I received a lot of stares.

I clutched the folder containing my documents tightly to my side as I found my way to the visa centre. A young man at a desk pointed down a corridor to a sign declaring I had arrived. Expecting to see a room of waiting applicants I discovered an empty room except for two young men sitting behind their computers. I wondered if I had come to the wrong office, but when I asked they assured me this was the place. I was very warm from the walk, and since the news broadcasts had begun to talk about corona virus, I was worried my temperature might be mistaken for a fever. But nothing was said of it, and in a strong Russian accent I was politely asked to hand over my documents. He tapped away on his keyboard a few times and then turned to speak in Russian to his colleague. Their conversation seemed serious, and I feared they would ask about my accommodation, but instead he turned back to me and began reading my forms again.

"You are hoping to enter Russia in early March?" He asked.

"Yes, on the 3rd," I said.

He shook his head, "This is not possible with this application. There is a Russian national holiday that will prevent your visa being issued in time."

My heart sank. "Is there nothing I can do about this?"

"Yes, you can pay extra for an immediate visa."

"How long would it take if I do that?" I asked.

"The application will be processed in four days, and you will receive your passport back within a week."

I was relieved at this, "How much will it cost to do that?"

"One hundred and eighty-eight pounds," he informed me. It seemed expensive, but I was happy to do whatever it took. I agreed and he continued to copy information from my forms into his computer.

Since he had looked through my details, I said "Do you think there will be any problem with my application? I would like to buy my air tickets as soon as possible"

"I cannot tell you this," he said seriously. "Your application and passport will be sent to London, we do not process them here. I cannot tell you whether you should buy your tickets."

I nodded my understanding, and once I had paid he issued me with a receipt. He underlined two of the numbers on the slip, "These are your tracking numbers, to get your passport back." I folded it away carefully and pushed it into my pocket. The whole encounter had lasted less than ten minutes and I was back on the street trying to find my way back to the car park. A light drizzle of rain had sent most people looking for shelter, and as I walked through the quiet streets I could still hear the sound of the young man's accent running through my head. It made the journey feel closer and I was excited.

The urge to buy my air tickets was strong, but I waited until I was sure my visa application was successful. I wanted to fly directly to Moscow, which would take about three and a half hours, and so chose British Airways flying from Heathrow. To avoid having to pay for a hotel in London I chose a flight departing at nine-thirty in the evening, which would give me a whole day to get down to the airport. It would mean arriving in Moscow at around four in the morning, but this seemed the best option. The cost of the flight was only a hundred and twenty pounds each way, much less than I had expected, and I realised the whole trip was not going to be expensive. When my passport was returned a whole page was taken up with an impressive looking visa that had been stuck in, and I realised there was now nothing standing in the way of the trip.

But the monasteries had still not got back to me and the thought of arriving in Moscow with nowhere to stay wasn't something I was willing to risk, so I booked a night in a very cheap hotel, just for peace of mind. In the meantime my Russian friend had begun to contact people in Russia to tell them I was coming. She began to send me names and contact details of people she assured me would be willing to help me out. She had even arranged for someone to meet me at the airport and drive me out to a monastery an hour and a half outside Moscow. I was overwhelmed by such kindness, but not knowing any of the people I wondered if they would really be there, especially so early in the morning when I arrived. But my friend kept assuring me that all would be well, "This is what Russian people are like," she often repeated, "You will see."

At her suggestion I also wrote to the office of the Patriarch in Moscow, asking for a blessing to stay at the monasteries and for suggestions about where to stay. A few days later I received details about the convent of Saint Mary and Saint Martha, as well as the suggestion that I contact the Pilgrim's Centre at the church of Saint Maron the Syrian Hermit. I was informed that they would know whether they could accommodate me soon, and would let me know in a couple of weeks. This would be just a few days before I was due to fly, and I began to grow nervous about finding last minute bookings if they couldn't fit me in. But with one of my bags already packed for the trip, they contacted me to let me know I could stay with them for six nights. The cost was just thirteen pounds per day, which I assumed meant it would be a shared dormitory or something similar, but with so little time left before I flew, I was just relieved to know there would be a bed for me.

The journey to Heathrow meant changing trains at Birmingham and Piccadilly, and riding the London Underground to catch the airport shuttle. By this time the Coronavirus outbreak was making more news and for the first time I saw people wearing medical masks. At Heathrow there were many more masks being worn, especially by young people. I had a number of hours to wait before my flight, and I sat watching the crowds come and go in response to the notice board which announced when and where we could board. Seeing a sign pointing to what was called the "Multi Faith Prayer Room" I decided to take a look. I leaned in through the doorway and found a bare room in which three Asian Muslims were kneeling on their mats. I walked away and returned to my seat.

By the time the flight to Moscow was announced the crowds had thinned out, and when I arrived at my terminal there was no one to be seen. Large television screens were announcing the latest numbers of people who had caught the virus, and it seemed everyone had decided not to travel. When boarding began the crowd of passengers had swelled to nineteen, and it took five minutes to get us all on board an aircraft designed for a hundred and fifty travellers. In his address the pilot informed us that once we were in the air we could sit anywhere we chose, and the majority of us moved from economy to business class. The level of comfort improved dramatically, and the cabin crew did all they could to persuade us to accept as many complimentary drinks and sandwiches as we would take. "They'll only be thrown away when we land if you don't have them," the stewardess told me, but sadly the feast on offer was mainly full of meat and we had entered Lent.

Watching the lights of cities pass beneath us I wondered what the trip would bring. Being alone gave me time to pray and reflect, and though I was tired, my mind was racing too much to allow me to sleep. I felt a deep sense of peace as we hurtled through the night sky, a peace that was only disturbed when the pilot informed us that we would be landing in Moscow in thick fog. "Visibility is no more than one hundred metres," he said, "so it is impossible to land manually. The aeroplane is going to land for us." As we descended I watched the flashing light at the end of wing illuminating the fog around us, and only when the runway was immediately beneath us was it possible to judge our height. We landed with a heavy bump but the usual relief filled us as we began steering towards the lights in the mist. At first sight, the airport buildings looked exactly like the images I remembered from so many old spy movies set in the time of the USSR, and the early morning fog only added to the impression. We gathered our belongings and said farewell to the British Airways staff as we entered the tunnel that had been fixed to the side of the aeroplane. At the entrance to the building we were greeted by a young woman in Russian military uniform, and as she carefully watched us go by, I knew I was now in a very different place.

Chapter Two

With so few passengers arriving we were able to quickly navigate the roped off lines that snaked back and forth up to the entry desk. Behind the glass sat a woman in her late twenties dressed in a uniform that carried as many badges as you'd expect to see on a five star general. Her epilates were crowned with large insignia that made her look more like a soldier than an airport bureaucrat. I slipped my passport through the slot along the bottom of the window and she began her inspection. She turned its pages beneath a large magnifying glass and studied the visa for a long time. I was confident all was as it should be, but as her inspection continued I began to become anxious. Eventually she looked up and asked my name. Her eyes were impenetrable, there wasn't a hint of emotion anywhere in her face to suggest whether this was normal procedure or if I should prepare myself for questioning in a dark room. I confirmed my identity and she returned to the passport. Eventually she pressed some buttons and produced a slip of paper which she proceeded to stamp. She slid them through to me and said nothing.

"Should I keep this with my passport?" I asked.

She nodded and stared back at me. With some relief I pushed the documents into my bag, thanked her and pressed through the turnstile that gave me entrance to Russia. I found myself in a corridor constructed of what looked like temporary walls on stands and followed the arrows that pointed the way. My friend in England had arranged for a Russian woman to meet me in a restaurant inside the airport, and as I walked I repeated the name to myself so that I could get the pronunciation right in case I needed to ask for directions. I passed through another security station where two men in uniform gave me little more than a glance, and I emerged into the main foyer of the airport. To my surprise there were still travellers milling around. What I didn't know was that the train service to the airport stopped running at midnight, meaning anyone catching an early morning flight had to kill a few hours at the airport, or risk catching a taxi. It was something that was to become more important to me a week later when it was my time to depart.

I walked over to an information desk where a young woman was talking to a soldier who was armed with a black AK47; having never seen one up close I forced myself not to stare in case it made its owner suspicious. The woman looked at me and smiled and told me in clear English to go up to the upper floor. An escalator carried me up to where at least a hundred people were sitting around, many of them trying to sleep. Along the balcony there was what looked like a market stall selling Russian dolls and other traditional souvenirs. I made a mental note of some of the prices, in case I wasn't able to find something to take back to my wife over the coming week. I couldn't see the restaurant and eventually approached a guard at a security entrance to ask for help. It was a shock to discover it was located the other side of the airport security, which meant I couldn't get back to it. I presumed the woman picking me up wouldn't be able to get through either, and I began wondering what I should do. I still had twenty minutes before we were due to meet, and decided to use the airport Wi-Fi to contact her. Not owning a smart 'phone I was disappointed to discover a password was needed that could only be received through one; frustration began to get a grip of me. As I glanced around I saw a sign pointing to the chapel, it carried a picture of an onion-shaped dome which felt reassuring. It was thirty seconds from where I had been sitting and as I entered I was met with the sound of two women chanting the night office. Their voices harmonised beautifully, a clear sign they had chanted together many times before. One of them came over to me to ask for a blessing and pointed to where the candles were kept. I lit a couple before the large framed icons that covered the walls, I thanked God for bringing me safely to Moscow, and asked for help in finding my contact. I stood for a little while to let their singing affect me; it settled me down and helped me to pray.

I decided to give the Wi-Fi another go and found a seat near the top of the escalator, hoping I would be easy to spot. I bent over my Kindle and began tapping away, but it was clear I wasn't going to get access. As a wave of anxiety passed through me I heard a woman's voice with a strong Russian accent say "Father Spyridon?"

I looked up to find a woman in her late thirties with long blonde hair standing directly in front of me, across her chest she held a large cardboard sign which had my name printed across it. A huge sense of relief flooded through me, and as I stood the woman held out her hands for a blessing.

"I'm so glad to see you," I said, "thank you for coming out so early."

"That is no problem," she smiled, "did you have a good flight?"

I shared a few details as I packed my things away, and seeing I was ready she said "Follow me to the car park." She led me down amongst the expensive looking cars to her own that was equally impressive.

"Should I drop this on the back seat?" I asked.

She misunderstood my question and said "You can sit in the back or the front, I do not mind."

"No, just my bag," I explained, "I'd like to sit in the front."

"Oh good, I was hoping to practice my conversation with you as we drive."

She reversed out from between the concrete pillars and steered through the narrow rabbit warren that led to the exit. There was little traffic about and the night was still thick with fog. She told me it had been like this in Moscow for nearly a week, but that it had been a warm winter.

"Zvenigorod is about ninety minutes, you can sleep if you want to."

"Thank you," I said, "but I don't want to miss anything." In truth I was too excited to sleep, and she seemed relieved at this as she pulled out onto a five lane motorway. Almost all the other vehicles were trucks, and when I commented on this she told me "They are only allowed to enter the city at night. During the day it is much better." They threw up thick layers of mud across our windscreen and there seemed no rules as to when and how they could pass each other. A number of times she had to swerve violently to avoid them but none of it seemed to concern her and I assumed this was what she was used to. Through the haze flashing blue lights kept appearing as police cars sped by, the focus of the chase never quite clear, and their presence seemed to have no effect on any of the drivers.

As we chatted I discovered she worked in publishing and she told me about the different writers she dealt with. When I asked she told me she would be working that day after she had completed the three hour round trip to drop me off. When I expressed concern for her she brushed it aside saying "I will get a couple of hours sleep when I get back to Moscow."

The thick fog meant I could only see what was immediately at the side of the road. We passed petrol stations and the kinds of fast food outlets that can be found alongside roads everywhere in the world; only the Cyrillic lettering reminded me that this really was Russia. Our conversation was relaxed and she very quickly told me about her life and her ambitions for the future. She openly admitted that she wanted to find a husband, and later when I told her that I had two sons I remarked "Then you are truly rich." A few times she asked me whether she was pronouncing something correctly and she was very interested in the occasional idiom I used without thinking. There was a seriousness to her that wasn't oppressive or cold, but at other times she laughed at the things we talked about. I asked her what she thought of President Putin, and she said "He is a good leader. He is strong, which is what Russia needs. We trust him because he takes care of us and of our country. When the Soviet time ended, there were many gangsters who stole from us, but President Putin took a lot back from them."

"The western media portrays him very badly," I said.

She laughed a little and said "We know this in Russia. But our media is biased too. As long as you understand this then it is possible to find a little of the truth."

"Is life very different now compared to when you were living under the Soviets?" I asked.

"Of course, in many ways it is completely different, some good, some not so good."

I was surprised to hear her say this, "What is not so good now?"

"The whole of Russia used to be productive," she said. "Everyone worked, all the farms were efficient, we did not have to rely on other countries for our survival. Since then there are many parts of

Russia which have been neglected. There is land which is not being farmed, there are resources that are not put to use."

"Do you think this is improving under President Putin?"

She pulled a face, "In some ways, yes. But there is so much to do. The US sanctions have been good in lots of ways, it has forced us to become more self-reliant again, we grow eighty percent of our food now, we don't look to other countries to take care of us. So the US and the EU are doing us a favour without realising it," she chuckled to herself at this and I admired her attitude.

As the early morning sky began to brighten we had left the fog behind us and I could see the passing towns and countryside. The buildings looked a mixture of traditional wooden, single storey constructions and more modern concrete multi-story flats. Many of the latter were grouped together, and looked to have been built in haste; they looked drab and uninviting and I pitied the occupants having to return to them at the end of each day.

Seeing me look at the buildings she said "There are many families that still have poor homes. The Soviets built the flats very quickly when the peasants were forced to move in from the countryside. They built them as cheaply as they could; it is still a rare thing to have your own garden here. But the effect of this has been that public spaces are very important in Russian life, and we take good care of them. But don't judge them only on the way they look on the outside. Many of the apartments are very nice inside. But yes, I admit that the buildings look ugly." She laughed to herself and added "My apartment is perfect, except I have no control over the heating. The administrator sets the temperature for the whole building, and I like it cooler than most people. But I can always open a window."

I hadn't expected to hear of this level of influence over people's daily lives, it was something I had assumed had gone with the Communists, but it didn't seem a big issue to her.

It was around half six as we entered the town of Zvenigorod. There were many typical old Russian houses along the roads, low structures that looked like they wouldn't keep much of the Russian winter cold out. No two were exactly the same, each had a different porch made up of fancy carved wood. They were something straight out of Doctor Zhivago, and I was pleased to finally see snow along the banks of the Moskva River that cuts through the town. "It's very beautiful," I remarked, "just like the pictures I've seen in books about Russia."

"It is a very old town," I was informed, "the first settlement here was built in the twelfth century. The people here are very proud of their history, but especially of their monastery. It is one of the most famous in all Russia."

It was the first time she had mentioned the reason we had driven out from Moscow to this little town of no more than seventeen thousand people.

Savvino-Storozhevsky Monastery is a spiritual beacon that shines out across the world, and suddenly I sensed how close I was to it. Eventually we pulled up next to a three-story modern building from which a woman in her early forties emerged. She smiled to see us and the two women began chatting in Russian.

"I am S.," she announced to me, "it is so good to see you Father Spyridon." She held out her hands for a blessing. "You must come in for breakfast."

I pulled my bag from out of the car and as I shut the door the woman who had brought me from Moscow announced "I will be heading back now."

I suddenly realised that without formality she was simply turning back to Moscow to face her day at work. "Thank you so much for your kindness," I said, "it has been good to meet you." The words felt inadequate.

"The pleasure has been mine," she said, "I am grateful to have had shared the time with you. And thank you for speaking to me in English." She received a blessing and after a quick exchange in Russian with S. she climbed back in and drove away. It was a little overwhelming to be treated with such kindness, especially from someone I would never meet again.

S. smiled and said "Please, come in."

I followed her into the building and down a plain corridor to a heavy security door that made me wonder if the crime rate demanded such a barrier. I commented on it and S. said "It is normal for Russians to go away for the holidays, so burglars know when apartments are likely to be empty. It is for peace of mind." She invited me into her little flat and in a hushed voice said "My husband is sleeping, he is working today. Please, put your bags in there," she pointed through an open doorway, "I will fetch you a towel and you can have a shower before breakfast." A bed had been made up for me in their living room, and as I took out toiletries from my bag I noticed a number of large paintings leaning against the walls. S. pointed me to the shower and it felt good to let the hot water wash away the grime of so many hours of travel. When I emerged I found her sitting at the kitchen table on which a number of plates and dishes were waiting.

"That feels much better, thank you," I said.

"Please come and eat, then you can sleep for two hours. After that I will take you to the monastery. When you have had time there we will catch a bus to Moscow. "

It was good to know she had planned out our day so well and I sat to eat. I was faced with a mountain of food: dishes of nuts, pumpkin seeds, sliced fruit and two plates of bread rolls. S. pointed to the bread and told me "These are from the monastery. They make them to sell to help keep it running." Pointing at one of the plates she said "These are filled with cabbage, and these are apple."

I noticed she didn't have a plate herself and when I asked if she was eating she said "No, no, this is for you. Please, eat."

"Are the paintings in the other room yours?" I asked.

"Yes, I will show you some of them before we leave. It is my job, I teach art at the school near here."

I broke open one of the rolls and found it filled with cabbage. It was sweet and delicious, more like a dessert than a savoury. I told her how good it was and she was clearly pleased. I ate as much as I could, but the lack of sleep had finally caught up with me. Sensing my mood S. encouraged me to rest, and showed me to my room. In bed I was too tired to absorb the reality of where I was, I had no sense of excitement or relief at having arrived, I was happy just to pull the clean sheets tightly around me and I quickly fell to asleep.

Chapter Three

I woke with a start as someone touched my foot and called my name. Sitting up I found S.'s husband standing at the foot of my bed laughing to himself. "Good morning Father Spyridon, welcome to Russia. I am going to work now, it is good to meet you."

As he left I glanced at my watch and found I had had just over two hours sleep. My body would happily have curled back into the sheets, but the sight of daylight streaming through the curtains was too strong an invitation to ignore. S. was moving around in the kitchen so I quickly dressed and washed and joined her there. She had already prepared coffee for me and as I sat to drink she said "We must go soon. Leave your bag here, we will return before catching the bus."

Outside she led me to an old Lada that she apologised about, and when I told her that I used to own one she was surprised that anyone in the West would be driving them. I didn't tell her that I had had nothing but problems with it. As we drove to the monastery she pointed out the churches and various other sites around town, and there was clearly pride in her voice as she began to tell me about the monastery.

"Do you know about Saint Savas?" She asked.

I admitted that I knew very little, only what I had quickly read on the internet before coming.

"He came here in the late fourteenth century and built a hut for himself out of mud and branches. He had a wooden church built dedicated to the Nativity of the Mother of God, but he remained in solitude as much as the people would allow. Today the monastery has many artistic treasures. The frescoes in the church are the originals from the fourteen hundreds, but the monastery itself has expanded and been renovated many times. The iconostasis that you will see was built in the sixteen hundreds, quite late compared to some parts of the church. Ever since sixteen-fifty when Tsar Alexis came here, all the Russian emperors have visited and prayed here. The road from Moscow to Zvenigorod that you travelled on last night was traditionally called the Road of God's Blessed Tsars. The people here are very proud of their history, our little town has always had an important place in the spiritual lives of the Tsars. Every one of them used to come here for a blessing at the monastery before they returned to Moscow to be crowned. Imagine that, here in our little town."

The road began to follow the course of the river and now there was more snow visible. The temperature had dropped in the last few hours and I was grateful when S. turned up the Lada's old fashioned heating system. Across the river were more of the single-storey wooden buildings and now it was impossible to spot any newer structures. S. became excited and said "Look, that is the old monastery wall." Ahead of us a high white wall marked the boundary of the monastery, and as we tuned off the main road she pointed again and said "That is the Tsar's gate. That is where they entered. But it is not used now." A Dark wooden gate stood closed and looked unlikely to be opened easily. Perhaps they will one day have need of it, I thought.

"People came from all over the country on pilgrimage to hear Saint Sava preach," S. said, "his sermons were very famous. And he performed many miracles in his life, many people were healed by him. You will be able to pray to him, at his relics in the church, his prayers still bring about miracles today. God is shown to us in His saints, and through their prayers He reveals His love." The simple and direct way in which she expressed her faith was moving, it was obvious how important it was to her.

We pulled up into a small car park and meandered our way through large puddles. The monastery gates before us were large and imposing, and through them walked a handful of visitors making their way to church. As we entered I could see the golden domes above the white church, and from within the singing of the monks drew us forwards. The monastery wall created an enclosed settlement in which various buildings of different ages sat around the church in the middle. There was a stillness in the air, a peace that I recognised from other monasteries; it was the profound sense of holiness that continuous prayer always leaves in a place. We walked quietly over to the church and crossing ourselves pulled open the door to find a large congregation of locals pressed together. The smell of incense and the powerful chanting of the monks immediately affected us, and as we entered no one turned their heads to pay us any attention, so engrossed were they in the worship. We collected a few candles and pushed forwards to light them before the icons. The Royal Doors were open and through the crowd I could see that the celebrant was a bishop. Around him hieromonks stood with bowed heads, their deep voices lifting the plea for mercy to God. I lit my candles and stared up into the face of the Mother of God. The icon depicted her tenderness towards her child and I was struck by their closeness. I began to think of how she had cared for Him as a child, how she had nurtured and protected Him, and I felt great gratitude to her for doing all of this for us. As my head tilted back I gazed at the ranks of icons that reached up to the ceiling and my eyes were naturally led out into the ancient frescoes that covered the ceiling and walls. The sense of being surrounded by the saints was vivid and immediate, and the great age of it all somehow pulled me out of any sense of now as a moment in time. It was like looking into eternity.

Deacons appeared at either side of the iconostasis and took their places before the Royal Doors. They censed the icons together, a synchronised action that looked natural and unforced. The sunken cheeks beneath their thick black beards signalled a disciplined life of asceticism, and I knew I was glimpsing only a tiny part of their enormous struggle. One of them proceeded to cense the people and then around the church, stopping before icons and relics to carefully reverence the holiness present in the physical reality around us.

When they had completed their censing, S. took my arm and led me to the relics of Saint Sava. She beckoned me forward to venerate him before her, and as I bowed to kiss the glass over his remains I knew these physical remnants from his life in the world were mysteriously connected with his life now in Heaven. I asked for his prayers and had to force myself to step away, so content was I to stand before him. We then made our way to the back of the congregation where a group of three elderly nuns stood with their heads bowed in prayer. I took my place beside them and allowed the rhythm of the Divine Liturgy to draw me into prayer. Despite my limited language skills the service was familiar enough that I could follow its progress and recall the prayers being offered. After the Gospel reading a short monk in black approached me. His long grey beard reached nearly to his waist, and without a word he offered his cupped hands for a blessing. Seeing a man who had so clearly spent many years seeking God now asking me for a blessing was a humbling experience, and as I always did in such situations, I reminded myself it was God's priesthood granted to me that made such a blessing possible, not anything I had achieved. As I blessed him he took my hand and gently kissed it, and with a small bow he turned and returned to his place somewhere unseen.

As some of the congregation began to line up to receive Holy Communion S. turned to me and indicated that we should go. I followed her out into the cold air and I could see she was looking for some kind of reaction from me. It wasn't something I had to fake to satisfy her, "That was very beautiful," I said, "thank you."

"I will show you around and then we will have a drink before we go." She led me past the church to an opening in the monastery wall from where we could see out over the fields and farms below. "All of this once belonged to the monastery," she said, "the monks have kept many families alive through the centuries. It has been important in the life of the whole town." We enjoyed the view for a few minutes and then headed to one of the little wooden buildings built against the monastery wall. Inside was a small bakers' shop with loaves of every size and colour stacked up along the shelves. S. pointed to some rolls and said "Those are the ones you had for breakfast." She chatted a little in Russian with the man at the till and then indicated that I should climb a wooden spiral staircase. The second floor was a restaurant, around the walls were small alcoves beneath intricately coloured stained glass. She ordered the drinks and refused to let me pay for them. As she carried them over to one of the alcoves she asked "Have you tasted Sbiten before?"

Sliding into the seats I said "No, I've never heard of it."

She placed one of the cups in front of me and told me to taste it.

"It's delicious," I said, "what is it?"

She smiled, she was happy that I liked it. "Sbiten is drunk all over Russia, you will find it everywhere. It is not really tea at all, it is honey and spices. It is very good for you."

We sat beneath a stained glass image of a tree, and as we sipped at our drinks and chatted about the monastery I admired the way everything around us had been crafted to be welcoming and beautiful. There wasn't a hint of plastic anywhere, everything was handmade from wood. This lack of artificial materials was a reminder of the people who had created everything there, it felt natural and human.

We returned to the car and on our drive back to her apartment she explained that parking in Moscow was too expensive, but the buses were very cheap. She said she would show me the pilgrim's centre, and then she would have to return to teach her classes at the school. Once more I was moved by the kindness of someone I had met that day for the first time, and I was relieved to know I wouldn't have to find my way round unaided.

As we collected my things we didn't have time to look at her artwork and we quickly walked the ten minutes or so to the bus stop. We stood beside a busy road and watched a digital panel counting down on the opposite side of the road. Eventually it reached fifteen seconds and the numbers turned to green, indicating we should cross. The colour changed once more once the countdown reached three seconds and then back to red to begin the whole cycle again. This system is to be found at almost all pedestrian crossings in the Moscow area, and I was very impressed by it. It meant that as you approach a crossing you know exactly how long you will have to wait, and it removes any sense of impatience as the numbers change before you.

The bus shelter gave enough protection to keep us out of the biting wind and within a few minutes S. told me our bus was approaching. I knew she was only making the trip into Moscow for my benefit and so I took out some money and insisted that I pay. She laughed and pushed past me to climb the steps up to the driver. When I asked him if she had also paid for me he nodded. As we sat she waved away my protest with a sweep of her hand and I felt a little embarrassed as I thanked her.

"You must get some sleep now," she instructed me, "I will sit there." She moved to the seat in front of me and I tried to rest. But Russia was passing by my window and I didn't want to miss a moment of it. It was good to have the time to be still, and try and absorb everything that had happened. Watching the passengers getting off I was struck by how poor some of them looked, and I watched them wander off into small towns along the way.

After about ninety minutes S. stood up and told me we were there. We stepped down into what looked like another small town, but this was the edge of Moscow where we would catch the Metro. She swiped her travel card at the turn stile and told me to go through. She swiped herself through and led me to a very steep and very long escalator. The Metro is much deeper beneath the ground than the London Underground but just as busy. At the bottom sat a middle-aged man in uniform watching to ensure everything was as it should be. He looked bored, and it was the first of many times I was to see men employed in what looked to be very unrewarding jobs that wouldn't exist in the UK.

We followed the crowd onto the platform which was a wide open space, with both sides open to each other. The walls were decorated with huge artworks rather than the advertisements that hang on every available space in the West. The slightly boxy train pulled up and everyone politely climbed aboard. There were seats for everyone, and the carriage was clean and bright. I was impressed with it all and it left me feeling very safe. The younger passengers had their eyes fixed on mobile 'phones, but there were a number of people reading books on the journey. I noticed that many of the men's faces had the typical wide cheeks and strong jawlines of traditional Russian appearance, and I was struck by the absence of anyone who wasn't white. After being in London this was something very different.

After a short ride S. led me across another platform and we caught a second train. Had I been trying to do this alone I would have ended up far from my destination and left to the mercy of the dreaded taxi drivers to get me back. From our stop we walked through a series of beautifully decorated tunnels that deserved more attention than we had time to give them. Once more I was struck by how civilised the whole environment looked, and how reassuring this was. We rode another escalator that was as equally long and steep as the one that had taken us down, and we emerged into the busy centre of Moscow. Traffic was heavy and the streets busy with shoppers and tourists. The buildings were set back from the roads creating a sense of space and light as lots of the sky was visible. Between two of the high buildings could be seen the golden domes of a church, the sunlight reflected off them and it reminded me that I was in an Orthodox country.

S. and I walked about a quarter of a mile along the street until we reached one of the gateways to Gorky Park. Its entrance looked like a Roman temple with a line of thick white pillars holding aloft an ornate stone archway. I knew the name from an old film starring Lee Marvin, and S. was pleased that it was familiar to me. We took photographs and from the steps she pointed out various buildings and explained what they were. I didn't realise that we were now very close to the Pilgrim's Centre, and what she was actually doing was giving me landmarks to use for when I was making my way around without her.

We crossed the road and followed a quiet street for about five minutes until we came to a two story wooden building, "This is it," she announced. I realised I could never have found it alone. Above the roof of the building towered the dome of the church beside it. S. took me to an unsigned door and without knocking let us in. It opened to a small office where a woman in her sixties was sitting reading beneath a poster of a nun. They chatted briefly and S. told me that she didn't speak English, but that she would take care of everything. Their conversation continued and the woman behind the desk opened a large file and began to read aloud from it. I wondered if my booking had been lost, there seemed to be some issue to be resolved, but the speed of their talking was impossible for me to follow. Eventually S. turned back to me and said "Six nights, yes?"

I was caught a little off guard, "No, five nights. I am booked into a hotel tonight, I'm not due here until tomorrow."

S. waved her hand in the way I had grown accustomed to, "You can stay here tonight, no problem."

I had already paid for the other room in advance, but with the chance to settle in here and not face finding the hotel, I agreed.

The older woman took us to the church. S. explained to me that all the keys were kept there. Inside was a small porch with a windowed door leading into the church. As we entered I could see that every inch of the walls was covered in frescoes. The ceiling arched above us and a large icon of Christ looked down from it to bless us. The church narrowed ahead of us and through the space I could see the ancient golden iconostasis before which a figure was cleaning the floor. An old man sat just inside the doorway before an open cupboard that was full of large keys. After a few instructions he handed the older woman one of the keys and she led us back out into the cold air. Around the other corner of the church was a two-story wooden building that a young man was in the process of painting. We climbed a set of wooden steps and she unlocked the main door and handed me the keys. I thanked her, and without any paperwork, she left me to it.

S. needed to return to work and said "I must go now. You understand that you can stay here tonight, and for six days in total."

"Yes, thank you for everything." I tried to let her know how kind she had been, but once more I was made to feel as though a huge act of generosity was nothing out of the ordinary.

She lifted the plastic carrier bag she had been clutching ever since we had left her flat "Please take it," she said. "It's the things you didn't eat for breakfast."

Without any fuss she asked for a blessing and turned to head back to the Metro. Another Russian I had known so briefly and who had made such a great impression on me was gone.

Chapter Four

Wooden stairs led to a spacious kitchen equipped with everything a large group of people would need. At the top of the stairs was a bathroom and separate toilet; everything was clean and new. My key fob was numbered twenty-five, and I walked down the dark corridor checking the doors for my room. Above the doors hung small icons, too high to kiss but they reminded me to cross myself before entering my room. It was furnished with a double bed, a desk and chair, a wardrobe and a small, empty book case. Above the desk were two large windows that filled the room with light, and I immediately opened them to cool the room down. The view outside was nothing more than another building, but sitting on the roof of its entrance was a large black cat that stared up at me as I peered out. I was glad of the company.

It was already late afternoon by the time I had hung my clothes away, and I sat at my desk trying to plan out how I would spend the next seven days. In front of me was a shelf where another row of icons had been placed and I was pleased to find Saint Spyridon among them. I began to pray but was disturbed by someone knocking at the door. I buttoned my rassa in an attempt to look reasonably decent and found the lady from the office with another woman.

"Father Spyridon," the woman I recognised said, "Please." She beckoned for me to follow. They took me to the kitchen where a tray of food had been laid out on the table. Next to it was a note in English:

Father Spyridon, I will speak to you later. The church service begins at six. I will see you then. P.

The two women nodded to confirm I understood the message. They smiled at my Russian as I thanked them and left me to eat. Before me was a bowl of dark soup, a plate of some kind of pulse that I didn't recognise in a grey gravy that looked very unappetising, and nearly a quarter of a loaf of sliced brown bread. Everything tasted delicious and whatever the grey gravy was made of, I was grateful for it. As I ate I read the short note once more and was relieved that there was someone I could speak to in English. For the past two years I had been learning Russian from CDs in my car, but I was quickly becoming aware of how little I really knew. Thankfully I had enough basic phrases to get by, and I was to notice that when people spoke in English, they often used the same phrases I knew in Russian: it must be the common approach to language teaching all over the world.

It is easy to allow fantasies to develop, and they can be dangerous. I had been harbouring one about this trip. I had imagined myself quietly saying the Jesus prayer and gently drifting round beautiful churches for a week. This fantasy was about to be shattered and the reality of the spiritual life would thankfully bring me back to my senses.

After washing the plates they had brought me I walked across to the church. Through the windows I could see the light of many candles and there was already singing ten minutes before the service began. Inside there were more than fifty people standing in prayer, the only light came from the candles burning before the iconostasis and the odd glow of light from candles placed before particular saints around the church. To my right an all-male choir was being conducted by a middle-aged man, there were only eight singers but the sound was extraordinary. I immediately wondered if I had ever heard better voices. As I lit my candles an old woman came over to me and after receiving a blessing began to speak quickly in Russian. I could understand very little of what she was saying, but it was clear she was explaining which saints the relics belonged to that sat in front of the iconostasis. There were around sixty relics in a highly decorated silver box before the icon of the Mother of God, and I was able to discern a few names amongst what the woman was saying to me, but they weren't saints that I was familiar with. I venerated them and stood back to one side for the service.

The congregation around me was evenly divided between men and women. Many of them were very elderly, and every woman and girl had their head neatly wrapped in a scarf. Incense was drifting through the half light, sweet clouds that curled around the pillars and arches of the church, filling the air with a physical sign of our worship. The first week of Great Lent is called Clean Week, a name which refers to the desire to enter Lent by cleansing ourselves of our sinful habits. To help us achieve this the Great Canon of Saint Andrew of Crete is served each evening from Monday to Thursday. It is a long service which was written as part of Saint Andrew's personal prayers, and it captures the spirit of mournful humility that characterised his being. Much of it is a dialogue between the saint and his own soul, an urging to repentance and reflections on examples from the Old and New Testament where men have sinned, and where God has been merciful. Though I could not follow the words of the service, I knew its themes, and as the choir captured the intention of Saint Andrew through their chants, I tried to reflect on how I had been living, and how I needed to change. Being so far from home, surrounded by people of a different nation, I felt vulnerable, and this helped to prompt me to plead inwardly for God's help.

During the service the priest comes out to chant from amongst the congregation, and here there were three. All of them had long hair tied back, and as the candlelight reflected on their vestments they took it in turn to chant the troparia. As the choir responded we made our prostrations. I noticed even the very elderly lowered themselves to the floor, and each time we prostrated everyone's foreheads touched the ground. After the first hour I began to feel tired and my body demanded that it be given rest. It prompted me to consider how little sleep I had had that day, and I began to make excuses for myself, and why I should feel more tired than anyone else. But one glance at the women in their eighties who were prostrating without complaint put my tiredness to shame. As my body ached, my heart was lifted by the choir, and I realised that just as one part of me had begun to long for an end, my soul wanted nothing more than for this moment to never end. I was struck by how universal that battle can be within us when we struggle for God, and how our bodily weakness can be the very tool by which we draw closer to Him.

The service lasted for nearly two and a half hours, by the end of which I could feel my back tightening but my heart rejoicing. As the choir finished chanting, the congregation moved forward, forming a tight group before the Royal Doors. One of the priests came out from the iconostasis and began to preach. As he spoke the people remained completely silent, and for fifteen minutes they remained this way. There was no sign of emotion in his face or voice, but I sensed that he was imploring us to struggle hard for the rest of Lent. As he concluded the congregation queued to receive his blessing and slowly drifted out through the church and back into the world.

The woman from the reception desk approached me with a younger woman beside her. The latter said "Father Spyridon, is everything alright with your room?"

"Yes, thank you."

"My name is P., if there is anything I can do to help, you may ring me on this number." She handed me a slip of paper with her name and number written on it as well as details for the centre's Wi Fi. "Do you require meals while you are here?"

"No thank you, I will take care of myself." I didn't want to be bound to a timetable without knowing what the structure of my days would be.

"Your room for six days will be seven thousand two hundred rubels, will this be alright?"

It worked out to about thirteen pounds a night, it was more than alright. After she had explained some of the practical details about the keys to me I said "Can you tell me where the nearest monasteries are from here?"

"Yes, of course, we have a tourist map in the office you can have. The monastery of Saint Mary and Saint Martha is about fifteen minutes' walk from here, it is not difficult to find."

I asked about service times in the church, and she ran through a long list, at least two services each day. I made a mental note as she led me out to the office. The street map was very straightforward and showed where all the local churches and monasteries were located. A. said goodbye to her and paid the older lady for the room. There was a calm in her eyes that gave her whole face a gentle expression, and it was clear that the effect of the service was still at work in her.

I stepped out once more into the night air. Now that the sun had gone down it was noticeably colder, every breath was like an icy finger in my chest. From the map I could see we were just a few minutes away from Gorky Park and so I decided to investigate it before going to bed. It was closer than the map suggested and at the gate I asked a man in military khakis what time it shut. He told me not until midnight, and I thanked him and wandered in. It was not as I expected. The Lee Marvin movie had led me to believe it was a wild and unkempt place, but in reality it was full of mown lawns, wide footpaths and many sculptures. It was too dark to get a good look at them, but I knew I would be back some time in the daylight. I walked over to the bank of the Moskva River. In both directions I could see bridges which were lit up with hundreds of tiny lights. They looked like something out of a children's fairy tale and I knew it was something my wife would have enjoyed seeing.

As I leaned on the wall looking down into the dark river another security guard walked by, equally stocky and tough looking as the one at the gate. In different times the sight of them would have created anxiety, but in modern Russia they are a reassuring sight. The night was very dark, it was my first night in Moscow, but it felt very safe and I was in no hurry to get back to my room. I strolled along the pathways for a while longer and then looked for the monuments that would lead me back to the right exit. One thing I was to discover about the whole of Moscow is that it is very difficult to get lost there. The skyline has so many unique churches and towers that there is always something to use as a sign of where to head.

The guard nodded as I passed him again, and I found my way back to the Pilgrim Centre. There were no lights on as I let myself in and it was clear that I was the only guest. I had the whole building to myself, without noise or the need to make polite conversation. I had packed a good supply of red bush tea and with a cup made I locked myself into my room and sent a message home to let my family know how things had gone so far. I sat for a while in front of the icons, and as the lack of sleep finally took its toll on me, I set the alarm clock for the morning and climbed into bed.

Chapter Five

The route to the monastery took me through Gorky Park and along the river. This was to be my routine for most of the next seven days. It was as simple as the map made it look and I was soon approaching the domed church of the convent of Saint Mary and Saint Martha which sat amongst the shops of a busy street. Even at seven in the morning there were lots of cars but just a few pedestrians. The entrance was easy to spot thanks to the large icon of Christ above it, and the doorway led in to a set of steps down into the church itself. It was surprisingly modern looking with two large side chapels where, in each of which, a handful of ladies stood in prayer. The main iconostasis was directly ahead where a congregation of around thirty people was already listening to the Gospel reading. The priest was in his early thirties, his beard and hair were short and he had a strong tenor voice. I waited until the reading was finished before entering and lighting some candles. The choir consisted entirely of nuns who sounded like angels.

Once more I was able to follow the Liturgy despite the short-comings in my Russian, but since I hadn't introduced myself I had no intention of approaching for Holy Communion. The familiarity of the service was reassuring, and I found it easy to pray. At the end of the prayers I joined the queue for antidoron, and was surprised to be given a cup of hot Sbiten with it instead of wine. As people began to leave I went over to one of the side chapels and prayed before the icons. There were relics permanently available to venerate, and the experience brought a deep calm into my body. Before leaving I checked a notice board and made a note of the service times. The time had passed quickly and I was feeling hungry. I went out to find a bench to sit on to eat one of the cabbage-filled rolls I had wrapped up before setting out. But there were no seats anywhere, and having failed to find one on this occasion, I would consciously notice everywhere I went that people were not encouraged to sit around in Moscow. I decided to eat once I was back in my room, and checking the map to be sure I had read it correctly, I set out for Red Square.

Less than five minutes' walk from the monastery the road stretches over the river across a wide, ornately designed bridge. Collections of fairy lights hung from the lamp posts, and were it not for the heavy traffic, the bridge would not look out of place in Disney Land. As I continued to walk I looked down across the river at the imposing sight of Christ The Saviour Cathedral which dominates the skyline from that side of the city. As I followed the footpath the multi-coloured domes of Saint Basil's Cathedral came into view. Perhaps more than any other image, they have come to represent Russia to the outside world, and as I approached there was a sense of unreality seeing something directly in front of me that I had seen in pictures so many times. I began to think about the countless saints who had visited and prayed there, and it was easy to feel connected to them as I walked the same road towards the temple. From the bridge there is a large open space before the cathedral. Directly to the left of which sit the red walls and towers of the Kremlin. Beyond the walls stood the green and white palace that had been a symbol of power in Russia for so long.

A policeman blew his whistle and waved his hand at a group who had wandered from the marked pedestrian route, and I imagined how different his presence would have felt to Christians here just a short time ago. Getting closer to Saint Basil's I began to see how intricately it was built, with ridges of brickwork in different colours decorating every available space. It looked like something from a children's sweetshop, and I marvelled a little at the audacity of the architects Barma and Postnik Yakovlev who created such a vision in the sixteenth century. Legend claims that Ivan the Terrible had them blinded after its completion to prevent them from ever reproducing it, so desperate was the Tsar to ensure his temple would remain unique. The idea is that it resembles the flames of a fire, and it is in fact a series of small churches tightly collected together around the central Church of Intercession.

Standing next to the cathedral, Red Square opens up before you, an enormous area enclosed on one side by the walls of the Kremlin and on the other by large buildings that mark the beginning of the old merchant quarter. Images from old news reels of tanks and missiles parading through the square before Soviet leaders made it seem oddly familiar, but the intense red of the walls and the beauty of the other buildings was unexpected.

I walked to the opposite end of the square, through the large crowd of tourist almost all of whom were clutching cameras or mobile 'phones. I stopped to look up at one of the clock towers when three Asian men approached me. They were the first non-white faces I had seen, and one of them sheepishly asked if I was Orthodox. When I confirmed that I was he asked if they could take their photograph with me. I didn't have the heart to tell them I was an English visitor, and after they posed with me and went off happy with their picture, I smiled at the thought of them showing it to their friends, not realising my true identity.

I returned to Saint Basil's Cathedral and decided to go in. A small kiosk sold entry tickets, and when I asked for one the woman behind the glass told me it was free for priests. I showed the ticket to the security guard inside and followed the other tourists through the narrow corridors into the various little rooms of the building. There were icons on display, but they were protected by large glass panels and it was not possible to venerate most of them. Despite the recordings of Orthodox chanting that was played through hidden speakers, the impression is very much of a museum rather than a church. I asked one of the guards if services were still conducted there and it was disappointing to discover that the temple was only used for its original purpose once a year.

On the second floor one of the ancient iconostasis was on display, and I stood for a while trying to bring to mind the many saints and bishops who would have walked through it. In reality the design of the cathedral's interior makes it unsuitable for large services, as it is really a series of small, separate spaces. But knowing how the Soviets had stolen the building from the Church in 1928, and had turned it into a museum as part of its anti-religion campaign, I thought it would be a symbolic act at least to reclaim it from what the atheists had done. In truth, despite its appearance, the interior was very disappointing, and I didn't spend a great deal of time there. The gift shop provided a few souvenirs to take back to my wife, and barely fifteen minutes after entering, I was back out in Red Square.

In the open space beside the cathedral two *Russia Today* vans were now parked and the film crew were setting up their cameras. I recognised one of the reporters from their broadcasts, who was being positioned with the colourful domes directly behind him. As I crossed the bridge I took some photographs and wanted to capture one with me in it. A young man was taking photographs not far from me, so I approached him and asked if he spoke English.

"I do," he grinned, "I'm from Yorkshire."

We laughed and shook hands. He was gathering images for an exhibition on Russian architecture, so I was confident he could handle my little point-and shoot camera. He was happy to oblige, and it struck me how strong the bond is between people of a shared nationality when we are far from home. As I continued back to my room I was disappointed to realise how completely I had entered the mind-set of a tourist rather than a pilgrim and I resolved to do something about it. I had come to Russia intending to make a pilgrimage and I had allowed myself to become a holiday-maker. I had a few hours before the Canon of Saint Andrew would begin again at the church, and I decided to set the time aside to read and prepare. Moscow is a stunning city, I didn't see a single example of graffiti, and no matter where I went, I always felt safe. But being surrounded by such an attractive environment I found it easy to be lured into a worldly state of mind, and knew some time alone was needed.

Chapter Six

After a few hours reading I started watching the clock and started preparing for the evening service. I wasn't feeling anywhere near as tired as I had been the day before, and as I entered the church with plenty of time to spare, there were just a few people who had arrived before me. The choir leader was running through some last minute preparations and as they rehearsed something the sound of the full mixed choir filled the church. The combination of male and female voices sounded far more complete than a single sex choir, and immediately I felt their singing lifting me to prayer.

I venerated the icons and found a discreet spot to stand in and stilled myself. My head was filled with many unwanted thoughts and it took some effort to regain my focus. The excitement of the day, the anticipation of the service, it all competed for my attention, and I realised that even after spending time alone in my room I hadn't really discarded the distractions that I had allowed to enter me.

The church was again very full by the time the choir began the service, and once more we followed the pattern of the Canon of Saint Andrew, with its sombre tone that invited us to see the truth of ourselves and repent. I had been reading through the service so that I would feel more closely connected with its themes, and as we began the series of prostrations I prayed that God would accept my plea for mercy. Vivid thoughts of Judgement Day gripped my heart, and I knew that I was lost without God's mercy.

Some of the younger worshipers were using mobile 'phones to follow the service, they studied the words with great concentration and piety, and I wished that I had brought my copy of the service with me into church. The time went by quickly, and though my body was once more relieved to be able to rest, I felt a longing for the prayers to continue. Just as they had the previous night, the congregation moved forwards to gather around the priest to hear his sermon. This time it was the oldest of the priests, and he spoke with great gentleness that conveyed his love for his people.

When he was finished and people had received his blessing P. who spoke English approached me.

"Father Spyridon, I would like to introduce you to Father T." she said. We chatted for a while until the priest emerged from the iconostasis, it looked to have been prearranged as he headed straight towards us. We exchanged a kiss in the tradition of the priestly greeting and he welcomed me to the church.

"You must come and have something to eat," P. translated for me, "I would like to talk."

"Thank you," I said, "I would like that."

The three of us walked out and around the church to a part of the adjoining building next to the office. P. and Father T. spoke in Russian together, and the priest ushered us in before him. A small table and four chairs sat in the middle of the room. Other than a few small icons, the room was bare, and as we entered the woman from reception came in through a door that led to a kitchen. Father T. gave some instructions which I presumed included setting a place for me, and she quickly disappeared again to finish preparing the food. He gestured for me to sit, and with P. beside him translating his Russian into English, and my English into Russian, we were able to communicate, if a little slowly.

He asked about which part of Britain I came from, and was very interested in how the Church was growing in the UK. When I asked him about his own parish church he said "Our temple is dedicated to Saint Maron, do you know him?"

I admitted that I didn't, and Father T. nodded, "Perhaps he is not known so much in Great Britain. He was a priest in Syria in the fourth century, he withdrew to the mountains to be near to God. But as is so often the case, many people longing for spiritual help sought him out. He performed many, many miracles, which was good for the people, and for us, but it meant the whole nation got to know about him. This kind of fame is not good for a hermit who only wants to be alone with God." Father T. smiled at this, but his expression became more serious when he said "He lived in the mountains near Aleppo, and we all know how the Christians suffer there today. It is no surprise to us what the world is doing to Syria, when great seeds are planted the demons come to try to pull them up. Syria has many great saints, but who knows what will happen to the Church there now." He became thoughtful for a moment, and it was clear he was moved at the thought of these things, but once more he began to tell me about their patron.

"Saint Maron was an example of true monastic living. His asceticism was the fruit of his understanding. He understood how this physical world must not be ignored when we pursue a spiritual life."

Just then our food was brought in and we stood as Father T. blessed the dishes. As we sat he pointed to the food and said "Take all of this for example. We know that before a football team can play in the final, it must pass through the early rounds. In the same way, anyone who wants to progress in the spiritual life must win in the early stages of their development. To reach the heights of spiritual growth that the saints demonstrate to us, we must be victorious over the basic parts of our lives." As he paused to allow P. to translate, he watched my face carefully, studying my reaction to be sure I had understood his point.

"Food is necessary for life," he continued, "but unless we overcome the belly we cannot even think that we have made a start. There is not a single person who has achieved holiness that did not fast. So if we want to know God, we must fast too." He looked at the food before us and waved for me to serve myself. "This simple soup, this bread, it is all a part of our spiritual ascent." He smiled, "It looks good, let's eat while it is hot."

As we ate he said "I tell you this Father, my greatest problem with these people in this parish is that they all want to be ascetics."

I was unsure what he meant, though I had noticed that there wasn't anyone in the congregation even slightly overweight. "Why is that a problem?" I asked.

"We must stay on the golden path, down the middle, turning neither to the left or the right. Of course we are to resist gluttony, this is well known, and the signs of overeating become obvious to everyone." He laughed at this, and patted his stomach to acknowledge his own eating. "But we are not monks, and we must not try to fast like monks. We have Wednesdays and Fridays to fast, we have Lent and all the other prescribed periods of fasting, this is enough for our salvation: beyond this we must not go. Too many of my people fall into the trap of wanting to do more. In confession they ask if they may have a blessing to fast also on Mondays like the monks do." He smacked his palm firmly on the table, "And I say no! Always no. It is turning from the golden path, and is more dangerous than overeating. When we set ourselves above our neighbours, when we secretly do more and think we are better than them, this is a great fall. I see so many times people coming close to this trap. To be overzealous is dangerous Father, let what the Church has commanded us to do be enough. We must remember that being boastful is not just a matter of what we say, we can be boastful in the heart while still making a show of being humble. But such outward shows are another topic all together; Saint John of Kronstadt said that God is able to save the sinners we are, but not the saints we pretend to be."

P. was translating quickly and I realised I was the only one getting through my food. I laid my spoon down and hoped that they would catch up. Noticing what I did Father T. chuckled to himself, "I must eat more and talk less," he said. "This is my weakness, I let my lips get away with me." P. looked embarrassed to be repeating this and her discomfort made me laugh.

"I speak this way of my people, but you know I am blessed to serve saints in the making. Never was a priest granted such fine people. They remind me that the belly can be dangerous. It is from here that the demons get so much help in their battle with us. And so many passions begin here. I have heard it said that we can both fall and rise through the belly. It can lead us into every sin imaginable, and it can be the means by which we struggle for Christ. None of us can ever pray properly if our bellies are over full. This is a fact. Not just the mind but the soul drifts into a cloudy state when the belly has its way. Such delicate discernment is needed in the spiritual life, Father. This is why we must find a good guide, someone who has learned through his own struggles how to avoid the pitfalls along the way."

He paused for P. to translate, and ate a little bread. "I will finish, Father, with one thing," he continued. "It is natural to eat, God gave us this need and also the food to satisfy us. We can say, therefore, that it is natural. But when we overindulge, when we fall into the sin of gluttony, what is natural becomes unnatural. This is true of so much of our sin. We turn what God gives us into something selfish, we disfigure what is natural. Of course we can say that hunger was introduced with Adam's fall, but it was eating that which was forbidden that was the act of disobedience that led to the fall. Fasting was the first and only commandment that God gave in paradise, and see how failure to follow God's command has brought pain and suffering. Overindulgence is a distortion of what is natural, and we can overindulge in so many ways. We may want more experiences, more friends, more money, more interesting thoughts, but we must learn to watch ourselves. Saint Maron withdrew to the mountains to restrain his senses, restrain his impulses. This is the message of his life, that watchfulness over our desires is essential if we want to be filled with God. Otherwise we are so busy filling ourselves with other things there is no room for Him."

I had finished my meal and Father T. fell silent as he consumed his soup. P. asked him something in Russian and he gave her a brief response. As he lay his spoon down in his empty dish he said "Let us pray and then I will show you something." We stood and he blessed us, and the woman from reception came back to remove the plates. She smiled when we thanked her for the food and father T. beckoned me to the entrance. Beside the door hung a notice board, a large proportion of which was covered in photographs. They showed the church interior as it was before the icons and frescoes had been restored.

"You see this," he said pointing to a photograph of a bare wall. "This was how the Soviets left our temple. They tore everything down and put a lot of effort into removing all the images."

It had been left like an old warehouse and I couldn't believe that such a beautiful church had once looked like this. Father T. said "We raised the money, the people here, their hearts loved God and loved His house. It is like a miracle to me that we have the church you see today."

"Was it a very difficult time for you under the Soviets?" The question seemed unnecessary as I asked it, but I couldn't think of much else to say.

"In some ways, yes. It is my opinion that though they did terrible things to God's people, and of course they were led by evil men, in fact many thought they were doing the right thing."

"You mean trying to wipe out the Church?" I said.

"Yes, even something so evil. I believe that many ordinary people who worked for the Soviets had accepted what they were told: that to free man they had to abandon religion. The cruelty that they showed was anger at something they thought was hurting people. This is the devil's work, to take something noble in people and turn it against God. It is this same distortion that evil uses to steal our salvation from us. We are all at risk when we do not watch ourselves. We think we are doing good, but unless we follow the Church's teaching, who are we to know what is good? Especially today, people want to trust themselves, they believe in themselves too much, it is a dangerous state of mind."

I recognised the truth in his words, particularly for myself and the culture back in the West, where self-reliance is seen as a virtue and the concept of obedience has been completely maligned. The very nature of freedom has been turned upside down, so that the slavery to our impulses and desires is portrayed as liberty, while self-restraint and overcoming of self is imagined to be misguided or even dangerous to our psychology.

We spoke a little longer and Father T. finally said, "We are serving the Pre-sanctified Liturgy tomorrow, would you like to serve with us?"

He had not asked to see any evidence of who I was and he hadn't doubted my ordination. I was moved by the generosity of his offer, but I knew my language skills weren't up to it. I thanked him and explained my reasoning which he accepted with good humour. I was also uncertain about doing so without asking his bishop for a blessing, but I didn't mention this. We both thanked P. for translating for us, and she in turn thanked us for the opportunity to share our company. Her husband was waiting for her in the cold as we stepped outside, and encouraged by the night air we quickly said our goodbyes.

I walked once more down to Gorky Park and stood watching the river flowing by. A brightly lit pleasure boat chugged past and I could make out the revellers on board. The bridges were lit up in either direction and the evening traffic continue to head into the city. Father T.'s words had affected me and I tried to apply what he'd said to my own life. We can so easily imagine ourselves as superior to past generations because of our technological advances, but the truth is they lived lives that inclined them to spirituality far more than our own. The great saints lived in ways few of us could ever dream of emulating, and yet we read of their heightened spiritual states and fantasise to the point of self-delusion. So many writers talking about theosis, when in reality we can barely live out the demands of ordinary Christian lives. It is necessary that we abandon the prelest of our modern world and accept the simple struggle to be obedient to God. Anything more than this is, as Father T. said, very dangerous.

After ten minutes or so the cold air began to penetrate my whole body and I needed to get back to the warmth of my room. Other walkers enjoying the park passed by as I quickly strode back to the Pilgrim Centre. In my room I settled down with a hot drink and after a little reading set my alarm so that I could be in the monastery for the beginning of the Divine Liturgy in the morning.

Chapter Seven

The choir of nuns was chanting the hours as I arrived at the monastery. They took it in turns to sing the verses, and the steady pace of their voices created a prayerful atmosphere in the church. The young priest was hearing confessions to the side of the iconostasis before an icon of the Mother of God. A small queue of those waiting to confess stood a small way off, their faces serious and heads bowed. By the time the priest was censing the church, around forty people had gathered and the choir was now singing the familiar tunes that can be heard in every Orthodox church, regardless of language.

The Liturgy was served with great solemnity, and though I wasn't receiving Holy Communion, I knew my heart had been brought closer to God through the worship. As the service ended and the congregation queued to receive the priest's blessing, one of the older nuns gently squeezed my arm, and I turned to find her looking up at me with a smile. Her round face was squeezed by the black cloth that bound her head, and I guessed she was in her mid-seventies.

"Hello," I blurted in surprise, "do you speak English?"

"A little," she said, "your blessing, Father." She extended her hands towards me and kissed my hand as I blessed her. I was quickly to discover her English was excellent.

"Would you like some tea?" She asked.

"Thank you, that would be nice."

"What is your name, Father? I am Mother D."

I told her who I was, and she made a small bow as she heard my name. She led me out of the church through the entrance porch to a small room beside the main door. A younger nun was already there, busying herself with plugging in an electric kettle. They exchanged a few words in Russian and the second nun gave me a small nod and turned back to prepare the cups. We sat at a small table barely long enough to accommodate the three of us, and Mother D. asked me about my home and the parish I served. When I told her our patron was Saint Chad she said she knew nothing of him and wanted as much information as I could recall. As I spoke she crossed herself several times and she listened intently to the description I was able to give of Saint's Chad's life.

When I had finished speaking she said "Our monastery is dedicated to Mary and Martha," and again she crossed herself to invoke their prayers that God might bless us. "They were women of great obedience to God, so humble that they thought nothing of their own will. I have been a nun for forty-six years and I am still struggling to learn the obedience that these two young women displayed in their innocence. Our Lord taught us through His example of how exalted true obedience is, but still we demand to do things our way, even to the point of risking our salvation."

The second nun poured the tea from a black pot and we each mixed in a little sugar to sweeten the dark liquid. Mother D. returned to her topic, "All of the scriptures teach us what joy is to be found in obedience. When we run to serve God and are obedient to every command he gives, we draw close to Him. But when we are self-willed we push ourselves away from Him. No man can ever hope to know God without obedience. Christ became a man and lived in obedience to His Father. Adam and Eve lived in paradise with God until they became disobedient. Do you see how central to our lives it is?"

I nodded as I sipped my tea. She paused for a moment, her eyes stared off into the distance as she gathered her thoughts, "Think how God loved Adam and Eve, He was their Father, how sweet it must have been to live so close to Him. But when they disobeyed Him their conscience rebuked them and they were afraid of Him. Who amongst us can imagine this? And when God asked them about their disobedience, He longed to forgive them, longed to reconcile with them. But Adam blamed Eve, and Eve blamed the serpent. Instead of repentance they tried to deny their guilt. There is something important here for all of us. When we fall, when we are disobedient, God first approaches us and gives us the chance to admit our guilt. Such love He has for us. He comes close to us and wants to show mercy. But how often do we turn away, deny our disobedience and fail to receive what He offers? So you see father, our disobedience results in misery. We can expect only pain in our hearts when we fill ourselves with disobedience."

She cupped her drink in both hands, looking over the brim at me with such wisdom and kindness that I involuntarily smiled. I felt like a child with his grandmother and in her eyes I recognised maternal love. She said "Unless we cut off our will, how can we stand before Christ and be at peace? He shows us His obedience even to death on a cross, and we presume to be self-willed over the most trivial of matters."

"Has life in the monastery helped you to learn obedience?" I asked.

"That is why we become monastics, to learn obedience. When we are young and our elder says no to us, we may become upset or angry. It is this response in ourselves that we must watch for and overcome. To learn obedience, like so many things in the spiritual life, is a matter of watchfulness. Unless we see what is happening within us we cannot make progress. And when we look with honesty at ourselves it is a frightful thing. It is a wonder the poor nuns don't run screaming from their cells when they encounter all that they have brought into the monastery in their hearts. It takes courage to do this, not everyone has the strength to face it. But unless we force ourselves into this battle we will go on being the play-thing of the demons. They whisper to us that so and so is being unfair to us, or that our obedience is harsher than someone else's. The demons prompt us to feel self-pity over all the injustices that we suffer, and that we should stand up for ourselves and demand to get our way. It is an old trick, Eve was tempted by the same lie; the serpent convinced her that it was unfair that God should deny her the fruit. So we must watch for these things in our hearts, and when we see them we must reject them as lies."

Her voice had become a little croaky as it dried out and she sipped at the now cold tea. She looked into my eyes and said "When we allow guilt to enter us, the demons may enter also. Like a free ride into our hearts they are carried by our guilt. We must listen to every prompt of our conscience, right down to the tiniest and most insignificant matter. Otherwise we have set ourselves up over God, we have declared ourselves to know better. What a shocking condition to put ourselves in."

The second nun said something in Russian that I couldn't follow and Mother D. responded in an equally impenetrable flow of Russian words. To this the other nun stood and after making another small bow to me left us alone. "She must help the priest in the infirmary," said Mother D., we have a few sisters in need of support."

I was still thinking about what she had said and asked "How can such demons be expelled if we do not know they are there?"

Mother D. smiled, "The Fathers tell us that it is no great thing to cast out demons. It is far harder to remove the passions from our hearts than it is a demon who comes to harm us. The priest can pray and the demon will be removed. But the passions are so rooted in us that it takes great effort, great struggle to eject them. This should be our real concern, not worrying about demons, but trying to remove the passions we have allowed to grow within us. When we sin, we fall. If we keep repeating the same sin it becomes a passion and our fall is all the greater because it is so much harder to get up. The passions are a poison, a spiritual poison, and it is we who willingly drink it. The only way we can stop poisoning ourselves is to be obedient to God. He gives us commands to protect us, to guide us away from these harmful mistakes. Do you see this?"

I assured her she had made her point well, and for a moment we sat in silence, both of us letting the impact of what she had said work through our hearts. Finally, concerned that I had taken up so much of her time I said "Thank you for sharing these things with me, and for the tea."

As we stood, Mother D. said "Will you come again? I would like to talk further."

"I can come tomorrow, there is a service at the church where I am staying tonight."

"Very good," she smiled, "we can talk a little about prayer. Or anything else you want to bring up. I have enjoyed speaking English, forgive me if I am rusty, there are words I have forgotten over time."

She walked me to the main door of the church and thanked me for coming. Outside the sun was shining and it took me a moment to adjust to the brightness. There was still enough left of the morning to visit one of the churches and so I headed towards the bridge over the river to visit Christ the Saviour Cathedral. As I made my way along the busy street Mother D.'s words filled my head and I thanked God for what might seem to the world a chance encounter.

Chapter Eight

Within ten minutes of leaving the monastery I was on the far side of the bridge walking towards Saint Basil's Cathedral. To my left along the river stood the imposing presence of Christ the Saviour Cathedral which rose above the other buildings. I asked a policeman which way to go and he politely pointed me down a set of steps to the busy road below that followed the course of the river. As I got closer the sense of the cathedral's size increased, and as I reached the trees growing around it I stopped and looked up in awe at its beauty. A lower structure of tall arches were crowned with clean white towers on which gleamed the five golden onion domes that reflected the Moscow sunshine like fiery lanterns.

I had seen old pictures of Moscow where the cathedral stood alone, but now the surrounding buildings had crept closer, but even so, nothing had been built too high to detract from its impact on the skyline. I knew it stood over a hundred metres tall, and there was a surreal quality to its reality; it seemed too wonderful to believe. It was a monument to men's faith, and a celebration of God's love. Tsar Alexander I wanted to express both his and the Russian people's gratitude to God for the retreat of Napoleon Bonaparte in 1812. The original design was full of Masonic symbols, and when the devout Nicholas I (Alexander's brother) came to power he demanded that these ungodly images be removed. The cathedral was so celebrated in Russia that Tchaikovsky wrote his famous 1812 Overture to welcome its completion, which occurred a year after he presented the piece to the public for the first time.

The original cathedral had taken over forty years to build, back in the nineteenth century, but in his spite Stalin had it torn down in 1931. The sound of the dynamite that turned it to rubble could be heard all over Moscow, and would be echoed in the destruction of many more churches all across Russia. Some of the marble from the cathedral was used in the construction of the Metro I had so admired. If the Nazi invasion had not distracted him, Stalin had intended to build a secular building in its place to wipe out even the site of such a monument to God, and above it wanted a huge statue of himself: but even through the evil that men do, God can act. The steel frame that had been built was stripped for the war effort, and Stalin didn't try again. A further act of God saw the Moskva River flood the building site to make it impossible to continue.

When the atheistic system of the Soviets came to an end, the memory of the cathedral was still strong, and rebuilding began in 1995, and was completed in 2000. While we in the UK only managed to construct a plastic dome to mark the millennium, Moscow had its cathedral back, much of it paid for with donations from over a million of

Moscow's Christians. As I admired all that it meant to the Church, I was also reminded that it was a monument to the failure of Communism and all its humanist philosophies.

I followed a footpath through the trees and came to an open space at the cathedral's base, it was surrounded with white walls made of large stone blocks, and I searched for an entrance to the cathedral. There was none to be found so I headed up to the main road past an entrance to the Metro, and there was the huge stone archway over the doorway. As I walked across to it a woman yelled out to me and I presumed she wanted a blessing. But her yelling continued and I realised she wanted money. This was the first beggar I had encountered, and as I fumbled through my pockets for change I remembered how I had been warned by so many people to be ready for streets that would be filled with the homeless. Perhaps this had been the case during the Soviet period, or after its collapse, but today there is little evidence of people having to live this way.

Inside the cathedral there was the immediate feeling of being in a church. This was not a museum or a worldly tourist attraction, this was a place of worship. I was immediately struck by the great sense of space, a carefully shaped mass of air that filled the distance between the walls of icons, the giant iconostasis, and the frescoed dome above it all. Individuals and small groups moved between the relics and the icons, lighting candles and praying. There were old women on their knees, some with their heads pressed against an icon, and most simply standing still, only their lips moving with the offering of their quiet prayers. The cathedral can accommodate a congregation of many thousands of people, and so it inevitably felt empty and quiet, even with perhaps a hundred people there.

The lower church is dedicated to the Transfiguration of Christ, and there are ancient icons depicting the event; so it was no accident that the completion of the cathedral occurred on 19th August. I had watched footage of the service of the canonisation of the Romanovs, the holy royal martyrs, the final imperial family murdered by the Bolsheviks. To be standing in that same location was very moving, and I prayed before their icons. As I looked up into the central dome I could see light pouring through the many windows beneath the final dome, and even above the light was Christ. The polished columns of marble would be astonishing in any other building, but here they served to glorify the icons around them.

I walked across to stand before the iconostasis and tried to imagine what it would feel like to serve the Divine Liturgy in such a place. Almost a complete chapel by itself, the iconostasis is built of polished marble and has a domed roof supporting a cross. The four tiers of icons draw the worshipper into the presence of Christ, His Mother, and many saints from the New and Old Testaments as well as more recent patriarchs. Unlike Saint Basil's, here the Divine Liturgy is served every day, in the chapels within the cathedral, and on many great feasts the Patriarch leads worshippers at the main altar.

I prayed for some time before the relics of Saint Philaret and then made my way towards the exit. I looked around before leaving, trying to absorb as much as I could. I thought about the many who had died at the hands of the enemies of God. Not those who were slain by Napoleon's canons, but the Orthodox Christians who had suffered persecution in Moscow even within many living people's lifetime. For such a cathedral to stand in this place would once have seemed a miracle to those dragged to their deaths at the hands of the Bolsheviks. I forced myself to grasp something of their perspective for fear of taking any of it for granted. As I crossed myself one last time I knew what a blessing this place was for Russia and for the whole world.

As I walked back towards the Moskva River I saw the woman I had earlier given some coins to. I was embarrassed to realise she wasn't begging but selling cloths and scarves. What I thought was an act of generosity on my part may have caused her great offense. I avoided walking past her a second time and made a wide detour. It was a warm day and it felt good to be walking alongside the river back to the bridge. But before I reached it a young man in his early twenties stopped in front of me and began speaking too quickly for me to have a hope of understanding. I explained I was English, at which he said "I am sorry Father, I wanted to ask an existential question." As I invited him to ask whatever he wished, I secretly delighted in such an encounter. The idea that a young man would stop a priest in the street and present his question in such a way would be impossible to imagine back in England. His query was far more down to earth than I had imagined, and when I tried to explain the Church's teaching on the matter he had raised, he seemed satisfied with the response and thanked me for my time.

At the bridge I stopped to gaze at Saint Basil's Cathedral once more, even though I had already visited it. There is something so outrageous and unworldly about its design that I felt compelled to walk around it again. It evoked a childlike response in me, something that defied the rational sense of an adult life. This uniquely Russian structure reveals something hidden in the national character. So often stereotyped as philosophical chess players with a taste for vodka, the cathedral reminds the world of a playfulness and an artistic sensibility that didn't conform to anyone else's judgement. If such a building were erected in London there would be outrage at committee meetings, and the architect mocked for his folly. But this playful collection of coloured domes has become the image of Russia all around the world.

At the other side of the bridge I found a small supermarket that stocked a good variety of vegan foods and it was with some enthusiasm that I carried my shopping back to my room. By the time I got there I realised that if I ate I wouldn't be able to receive Holy Communion that evening, but as I hadn't eaten anything more than a single cabbage-filled roll, I allowed my stomach to dictate my actions. The food was very good, but even as I chewed I knew I had made the wrong decision, and when I had finished I regretted my choice. I tried to convince myself that since it was Friday I could wait until Sunday before receiving communion, but I knew that I had wasted an opportunity for the sake of satisfying a little hunger.

I read for a while, and feeling annoyed with myself decided to go into the church to pray while it was quiet. Without a congregation present I could see far more of the frescoes and their impact was profound. The blues and golds gave life to the building, and the holy images stirred the heart. As I was lighting a candle an old woman who had been on her knees scraping wax from the floor, abandoned her work and slowly approached me. She spoke in Russian, and through the few words I could understand I realised she wanted to show me some of the icons. She led me round the church, naming each of the saints and giving me time to venerate them. She spoke in a matter-of fact tone that gave the impression she had done this many times before. Attached to many of the icons were small circular frames containing relics. Eventually we reached the back of the church and she led me to a large icon of Saint Spyridon. My heart leaped to see him, and it was with joy that I venerated his relic and asked for his prayers. I told the woman that I was blessed to be named after him and despite my poor Russian, she seemed to understand. She crossed herself and kissed the icon too, and the saint whose incorrupt body I had once visited in Corfu now felt close there in Moscow.

Once the tour was complete she left me to pray alone, and standing in the shadows beside an icon of Saint Seraphim of Sarov I was able to settle myself and open my heart to Christ. I recalled the names of the members of our community in Shropshire, then family members and old friends. I still had a couple of hours before the evening service and I tried to reflect on the expectations I had come to Russia with, and whether they were preventing me from seeing what God was actually doing with me. So often, even what we think of as positive ideas can become a barrier to the reality beyond our minds. We can force a subjective experience onto what God reveals and end up failing to see what He wants to do with us. I sifted through the conversations I had had, the people I had encountered, and I tried to assess what had been going on within my heart through it all. I realised that I still had a lot to let go of, and as Mother D. had said, if I was to be truly obedient it would mean obedience even at the level of seeing and experiencing the truth of my existence, an obedience in submitting to the mind to God.

I knew the service that evening would be long, and after a day of walking decided to rest a while. With a hot tea I sat and read from The Philokalia, and there discovered answers to questions I had not yet begun to consciously ask. By the time I had to return to church I could feel the longing within me to participate in the worship and I walked quickly under the darkening sky.

The church was once more filled with a large congregation, and two of the younger priests were serving with Father T.. The choir lifted words to God that were from all of our hearts and the sober delivery of the priests echoed the words of prayers offered by so many generations before us. Knowing how the Communists had defaced the church, I sensed the combination of both sorrow and joy in the worshipers, their gratitude to God was tempered with the history that so many of them had endured. At the sight of the chalice in the procession I knew Christ was once more giving Himself to His people and again we witnessed the realisation of God's love for us.

The long service passed quickly and as with every other service I had attended there, one of the priests came out to deliver a sermon. He spoke without notes for more than fifteen minutes, and the congregation listened carefully to every word. It was moving to see the honour with which they treated him. When he had finished I was about to leave but Father T. and his translator caught up with me and invited me to join them again for some food. I wasn't hungry, but I wanted to spend time with him and agreed.

"The other priests will join us soon," he said as he led me to the room we had eaten in the evening before. "What do you think of Moscow?" He asked as we sat down at the table.

"It is a beautiful city, I didn't know what to expect before I came."

"There are many problems here, just like in every city," he said, "but President Putin has helped Moscow to become a good place to live. For the majority of people it is probably a better time to live here than it has ever been, dare I say, even under the best of the Tsars there were people who went hungry. The people are important to our president, we believe that he cares about our nation. We are grateful to God for all that he has done."

"And he has done a lot for the church?" I said.

"Most certainly, you will have seen new churches being built, people are free to live their lives as Christians, and the Church is able to influence our culture and society in positive ways. President Putin has made all of this possible. I have been in attendance at two events when President Putin spoke. One was a meeting of the clergy and I tell you, the way he spoke, it was impossible to say whether we were listening to a priest or a president. His heart is truly Christian, thanks be to God."

As he spoke the two younger priests arrived and they greeted me with a kiss. They spoke no English and Father T. spoke to them, looking my way every so often which indicated he was explaining who I was. The youngest priest asked me something and I looked to P. to translate. "You are Russian Orthodox?"

"Yes," I said, and after a little hesitation told him "I used to be under the Patriarch of Constantinople."

"Was your move prompted by the situation in Ukraine?" He asked.

I nodded, "Yes, my conscience wouldn't allow me to be in communion with schismatics. But the Russian tradition has always attracted me."

"It is a grave business," said Father T., "but most Russians, if I am honsest, have little interest in what the Greek Church gets up to. When they start to interfere in our territories it is a different matter, but Russia is big enough not to have to worry." He smiled to himself as he said this.

"Forgive me if this is something you would rather not talk about," I said, "but how do you see all of this being resolved?"

"Two Romes have fallen," said Father T., "but the third will not fall. Moscow can stand up to any outside attacks, even from American money." Before P. had a chance to translate, the other priests chuckled at the comment, and I was glad to see this level of self-confidence amongst them. "But politics is not the business of priests, we have enough to deal with without concerning ourselves with the power struggles of men. Let them fight over their land and their gold, we have a treasure far more worthy of our concern."

Bowls of soup were placed before us and Father T. said the blessing. It was a tight squeeze fitting all four priests at the table and I wondered if P. had refused to eat only to allow room for myself. But she was adamant that she would eat later. As we passed the bread to one another, one of the younger priests said "Are you married Father?"

I assured him that I was and he nodded his approval. "It is important to have a wife," P. translated with a slight blush to her cheeks, and I wondered if she had repeated exactly what had been said.

Father T. sat upright and let his spoon rest in his dish, "Our holy monks live like the angels," he said. They have overcome nature to be closer to God. But too often I have to tell people to give up on ideas of going to a monastery. Instead I say get married and have children."

I was surprised to hear him say this, and he must have recognised a quizzical look in my face. "We need monks, of course, the world could not continue without their prayers. This we believe and know. If there was no longer a monk in his cell perhaps God would end the world. Like Abraham pleading for the whole city for the sake of one just man. "The other priests nodded their agreement as he spoke. "But Father," he looked directly at me, "have you heard of Archimandrite John Krestiankin?"

"No," I shook my head.

"He was a lover of monasticism, and he knew the spiritual heights that such a life can bring us to. But so often when young people approached him he would refuse to bless their wish to enter a monastery. He often reminded them that the world and the Church needs children. If all our young people become monks, our churches will quickly be empty. And the monasteries too; he reminded the young people that holy monastic saints need parents too. But one thing, he would never bless a couple to be married if there was more than five years between them."

He resumed eating his meal, and I caught P. looking at him with great admiration. As he wiped his mouth and beard with a napkin he grew serious. "The West has rejected monasticism to a great degree. But I see that it has also begun to reject marriage too."

"People still get married in England," I assured him.

"Yes, of course," he said, "but there is a shift in the culture. I have read of artists and cultural figures calling marriage unnatural. They say that since we are living longer than our ancestors, marriage is no longer a suitable way to live. Even western psychiatrists I have heard saying similar things."

I knew that it was true and I nodded and said "Especially over the last couple decades. People have less expectation that marriage will last."

"It is a tragedy," he said. "This disruption is very harmful to all of us. Marriage was given by God, our Lord blessed the wedding at Cana with His presence. The scriptures and the Apostles witness to the sanctity of this way of life. It is one more sign of men using science to fulfil their own desires. Marriage is hard, it is harder to live with some Russian women for fifty years than any burden the world can lay on us." There was laughter all around the table as he spoke. "And who could dare to say it is easy putting up with us?" He prodded his finger at his chest. "But this is a holy struggle. God gives us a spouse so that we may learn to be patient, kind and forgiving. Once the romance of youth has passed there is a fine wine kept until last. We have a responsibility to the one we marry to help them find salvation. On Judgement Day we may be shocked at how closely our salvation is bound up with our wife or husband. It is a mystery, a union that is unique in its nature. Christ spoke of His own union with the Church as being like a groom with his bride. Such a lofty comparison tells us of what a holy endeavour marriage is."

"What about divorce?" I said. "How does the Church here in Russia view people who divorce and remarry?"

"Of course, the Church understands human weakness. Moses was told by God that we may divorce on the grounds of adultery, and since then we have accepted even other circumstances where this may happen. But as the Fathers say: God blesses a first marriage, permits a second, endures a third, but forbids a fourth. Such is His compassion to us sinful creatures. Of course, a priest may only marry once, but that is because just as the monastics are called to a higher state of living, so too we make additional demands of our clergy. This is only right. But even amongst the laity a second or more marriage should be an exception, and thankfully amongst Orthodox it remains so."

He turned to look at P. and thanked her in Russian for her help. She humbly bent her neck and they exchanged a few words. We stood and Father T. led the prayers. There was great affection in our goodbyes and I knew how blessed I had been to encounter them. I went back to my room and turned on my Kindle to send a message to my wife. I was in the habit of summing up each day to her before bed, and after that evening's conversation I was particularly keen to make contact. Amongst the messages was one from a Russian couple my friend in England had put me in touch with. They wanted to arrange a tour of the Kremlin and also of a museum just outside Moscow. If it was convenient they wanted to meet me on Saturday evening to discuss the arrangements. I gave them the address of the Pilgrim Centre and confirmed our meeting.

I now had just three full days left before the flight home on Wednesday. The sense of my time there slipping away prompted me to resolve I didn't waste a moment that was left. I checked that the alarm would wake me in time for the Divine Liturgy at the convent, and once in bed I was asleep within a few minutes.

Chapter Nine

Even in the early morning traffic the flashing blue lights of police cars punctuated the movement of vehicles rushing by just as they did throughout the day. At the sides of the roads, burly looking men in heavy, military-style uniforms took down the details of errant drivers; a public warning that kept other drivers in check. I walked quickly to the convent, partly because I was eager not to miss the beginning of the Divine Liturgy, but mainly because the sun had not yet risen high enough to chase away the cold of the night and I wanted to stay warm.

The final verses of matins were being sung as I entered the church, and the congregation was small. As the priest busied himself with the censing, he stopped and quickly bowed to me before waving the censer towards me. The rose-scented smoke clouded over me, awakening my senses to the coming act of worship. I watched an elderly lady dressed in black venerating the icons, only her head scarf distinguished her from the nuns. Standing before the Mother of God she paused for some time, and I sensed the conversation taking place between her heart and our Blessed Queen.

Once more I was not receiving Holy Communion and I recognised in myself an absence of something. When serving the Divine Liturgy there is a sense of movement towards that moment when we receive Christ into our bodies. The momentum of the service carries towards that unique, mystical union when Christ transforms us with His presence. Being present when this miracle takes place, and the simple gifts of bread and wine are transformed by the descent of the Holy Spirit, is a treasured blessing, but my soul and body longed to eat and drink God's offering of Himself. During some of the hymns I became a little distracted at the thought that the following day I would receive communion, and I began to consider how I should prepare. Seeing my thoughts wandering this way I made a decision to spend time that evening preparing for confession, and once this decision was made I was able focus on what was happening.

We queued at the end of the service to receive antidoron and I noticed Mother D. looking at me. She smiled and I remembered her promise to meet again. I hoped she hadn't forgotten or been given some task that needed her attention, and I returned the smile. After the prayers of thanksgiving she walked towards me and invited me for tea. I thanked her and followed her to the same little room we had sat in before.

"Please, sit down," she said, "how are you?"

"I'm well thank you, it's good of you to give me some of your time again."

She pulled a face, "Not at all, I am grateful that you have come."

As the kettle began to boil another elderly nun entered and the two of them spoke in Russian for a minute. Mother D. introduced her, but I didn't quite catch her name. She sat at the little table with us and Mother D. poured us all a drink.

"You have come all this way to Russia," said Mother D., "it is not just for tea. What would you like to talk about?"

"You said we could talk a little about prayer," I said, "that would be helpful."

"Yes, of course. This is the business of a monastic, what would you like to ask?"

I hadn't come with any questions prepared, and I hesitated for a moment. But then I remembered the pilgrims who had visited the Desert Fathers and said "Could you tell me something about the Jesus Prayer?"

The nun whose name I didn't know suddenly began speaking, and when Mother D. answered her I got the impression she was summing up what had been said. The second nun nodded and in Russian repeated "The Jesus prayer".

"I presume you say the Jesus Prayer already, is there something specific you want to ask?" Mother D. said.

"I do, but anything you can tell me would be helpful. Even something you might say to a complete novice," I said.

She laughed, "We are all beginners when it comes to prayer. If someone starts to think they are an expert then they are deluded. Saint Anthony in the desert used to say that every day he began prayer feeling like he was just starting out – and look at the heights he reached." She immediately began explaining what she had said to the other nun, and this was to be the pattern of our whole conversation. I didn't mind at all, it gave me time to think about what she had said, and allow any questions I needed to ask to formulate within me.

"Let us think about how we first go about it," Mother D. began. "We must begin by stilling our self, alone in our room, clearing the mind of the chatter of the world. When we start to say the words they must come from our heart as a cry to Jesus, not audibly, but in our mind. We must follow every word carefully, concentrate our whole being on the meaning of every utterance. The demons will try to prevent us, they will remind us how uncomfortable our stool is, or how little sleep we've had, they will do anything to distract us from the prayer. This is when we must be brave, we must force ourselves with all our will to pray. We must take the Kingdom by force!"

As she translated herself the other nun began to speak and Mother D. fell silent and nodded. She turned back to me and said "Mother reminds us that the name of Jesus burns the demons. It is too much for them to bear. So no wonder they want us to stop."

I nodded and thanked them both. "Should we say the prayer silently or aloud?" I asked.

"Both," said Mother D., "it depends on the circumstances. When our minds become tired and distracted, it is useful to say the words aloud, it helps us to concentrate. It can keep us from falling asleep! But at other times it may be the other way round. We can become tired from saying the prayer and so repeating it mentally is better." She paused to explain what she had said and then continued "We must be careful. Especially when we are new to the prayer. We can become distracted by the sound of our own voice. We begin to notice little things about the way we are speaking, or how the words feel in the mouth. When this happens it is better to say it mentally so that we don't distract ourselves from the meaning of the words. If we think we have a nice voice or we just start beginning to enjoy hearing our self saying the prayer, we can fall into vanity. Our attention must be on the words, but also on ourselves, what it is we are allowing to move in our hearts. There is a stage we may reach when the mind finds such delight in the prayer that there is no longer any need for the lips, and the prayer begins to become a continuous presence within us. The joy it then brings is very sweet; such a simple blessing that can sustain us through so much."

During her translation I sipped at my tea and knew that she had been speaking about something that was the reality of their lives. I had been right to ask for something suitable for a beginner, and as her attention returned to me I said "How can we overcome distraction? So many thoughts drift into my mind when I am praying, I keep having to bring myself back to the prayer."

Mother D. nodded knowingly, the question was nothing new to her. "When we set out on the road of the Jesus Prayer, no one at the early stages can rid themselves of unwanted thoughts without God's help. When our minds are being led into captivity we must cry out to God to save us. The more we call to Him, the sweeter the prayer becomes, it warms our hearts, and the demons cannot bear this. The more we turn to Christ and plead for Him to help us, the further the demons are driven from us. This has been the experience of many saints throughout the ages. They have struggled like us, and they have told us what is effective in overcoming our enemies. They give us the map for the journey, and if we follow their guidance we may tread in their footsteps. Saint John Climacus tells us that the name of Jesus is a fire that burns the demons, and he says we should use Christ's name like a whip to scourge them and drive them from us. When we do this and experience the reality of this teaching, it encourages us, our hearts respond because we learn that this is not some theory, but the truth that has been lived by many."

As she began speaking in Russian I had time to think. I began to wonder about thoughts themselves. I was not sure if the cause of all my distractions was demonic, and when the opportunity came I said "Where do these thoughts come from Mother D.? Sometimes I think they come more from me than from the demons. Am I right to think this?"

"Our minds were created simple," she said. "God gave us the capacity to focus on Him and so grow in holiness. But we have divided our minds. The memory of God is sometimes lost in a multitude of thoughts, and so our task is to return to this simplicity."

"How do we do this?" I asked.

"Simplicity of thought is the remembrance of God. To focus our minds always on Him. But we are weak, our minds chase after the most superficial and carnal ideas that the demons suggest to us. And so we must pray. The Jesus Prayer is the means to achieve this simplicity. It unites our mind to God through His grace, God leads us back into simplicity. When the Holy Spirit works within us He heals our memory."

"I'm not sure what you mean by this," I admitted.

"It is the same as simplicity," she said. "We were created to remember God, to focus on the virtues. But our memories bring before us all the filth and silliness that can be found. It is darkness, and God cleanses our memory by uniting Himself with us. He is light that fills the soul, and the darkness of these memories is driven from us. Light and darkness cannot exist in the same place. When we fill ourselves with one, we expel the other. God's purity cannot be found where there is evil and filth. So too His purity makes us clean and washes away the stains of our sins."

She had begun to speak with a greater firmness in her voice, not louder or quicker, but there was a certainty in her tone that gave her speech the sound of great authority. I felt she was combining the teaching she had received with her own experience; she spoke as one who knows.

She became even more focussed and leaned forwards, "Let me tell you something about the demons. They come in disguise. They dress themselves up in all kinds of images, and in their cunning they know exactly which will work on us. Whatever passions we have within us, they bring their suggestions just for us. It is very personal, very specific to each of us. Their aim is to feed the fire that already consumes us. They prompt us with just the right fantasies that tickle our lust, or our vanity, or our anger, or whatever it is that will work in us. They have spent many centuries getting to know human psychology, they have caused many to fall. We must fight so that we don't become their next victory."

As she explained herself to the other nun they began to converse in Russian and at first I thought there was some disagreement between them. But Mother D. eventually explained everything to me; "We are wondering how much we should talk like this, but since you are a priest we are happy to say everything." She looked back at her friend and then to me, "When the demons attack, they work like an army, so that some of them will be in the front, others bring up the rear. First they suggest fantasies, almost like daydreams, they get us to engage with these until they can prompt the passions. Once the passions are stirred the demons themselves move in. And let us remember that the passions can operate in both the body and the soul, there are many kinds of passions; when we permit sins to be repeated they take root in us. We are so foolish at times, it is a wonder that God can be so tolerant with us. Such defiance and rebellion, we are a scandal, but still He loves us." She became emotional at this, and as she relayed her thoughts in Russian she crossed herself and the other nun nodded in agreement.

"Without His grace we could do nothing," I offered.

Mother D. thought about what I had said, such an obvious statement was given her entire attention and she said "We can practise all the virtues but unless God's grace is active in us they will not become a true disposition of the heart. Nothing truly transforms the heart except God's grace. Even a virtuous life will be dead if there is no grace. We may see someone and marvel at how many virtues their life seems filled with. But without grace it is nothing more than an illusion, a phantom, a mirage. Do you understand this?"

"I'm not sure," I said, "I'm not clear what we mean by the virtues if they can be like this."

"That's because our worldly thinking sees all virtues the same. Very few people can discern their true nature. I am not claiming to have such a gift, but there are those who can. Think of it like this, there are some virtues that come from our actions. When we will to do good and seek to please God. There are others that we might call natural, they come from our disposition, and may not be anything we have chosen at all. A person may be friendly or kind, simply because they have been brought up that way or been blessed to have been shown such kindness all their life from God-fearing parents. But there is a third kind of virtue, that comes from grace and is Divine. These last sort the Fathers called supernatural virtues, and they exist only through the work of the Holy Spirit. They exist in people only through the work of God in them. They are the virtues of the world to come. Even now, in this earthly life God grants us glimpses of the things that belong to eternity. So that eternity itself is here and now, found in these virtues in the hearts of holy people. These saints live for the true life which is eternal, and even in our dark age there are still such people. The world is permitted each new day because the prayers of God's saints call for mercy for all of us. And we must join our voices with theirs, pray that God will be tolerant enough for us to have one more day to repent. Russia has endured so much, but no matter how hard the demons have worked against her, there have been enough holy saints that God has chosen to preserve our nation."

"Mother D., will we all be like them in the world to come?"

"Of course, everyone will exceed what is done here in this life. But still these holy people will exceed us there too."

"Can you explain what you mean by this," I said. "In what ways will they exceed us?"

"You have heard Jesus say that there are many rooms in His Father's house. By many rooms He means many degrees of existence. We enter the Kingdom in various degrees of deification, with different virtues, and so our reward will be different too."

"Isn't the Kingdom of God one?" I said.

"Yes, but like this world there are different ways for us to experience the light. The moon is dimmer than the sun, and the stars provide even less light for our world, we can say that each possesses a different degree of glory. And so too those who enter God's Kingdom will have different degrees of glory, since we do not equally reflect the image of Christ. And just like the stars, the moon and the sun all shine in the same firmament, so too the blessed will exist in one Kingdom."

"I understand," I said, "and this will be both in the spiritual and bodily nature of man?"

"Yes, the resurrected body will be incorruptible, but still earthy, it will no longer exist only for the earth, but made for both earth and heaven. It will become as it was intended when it was first created; resurrection will be deification, conforming us completely to Christ's image. But this deification will be in accord to the degree of a man's perfection in this life. Do you see how important our earthly struggle is? We do not wish only to be granted pardon for our sins, but rise to the very image of Christ. Such limited western thoughts have stunted the spiritual lives of so many people. When our salvation was reduced in the minds of men to a judge deciding guilty or not guilty, the glorious plan of God was abandoned by such people. This is why Orthodoxy is so different to other kinds of Christianity. The heights to which God calls us are only to be found in the Church."

I felt this vision of our purpose grow within me as she spoke, and my heart clung to the truth of her words. As she once more shared her thoughts with the nun I swallowed the last of my tea. I knew time was moving on and I didn't want to outstay my welcome, but while I had the chance I needed to ask her one more thing. "Mother D., I was once told that there are few if any great saints left on earth. What is your thought on this?"

Her eyes glistened as she smiled and she patted my hand gently, "There are saints amongst us even today. There are still those who cannot do evil or even think of anything evil. Saints who are so filled with the Holy Spirit it is miraculous sometimes to hear them speak. God still blesses our world with their presence. But the world is changing. God would once have revealed these people to the whole world, and many would flock to them for a blessing. Many saints, even hidden away in the forests of Russia, were revealed to the world, and God touched the lives of many through their holiness. Today's people find it hard to be around such holiness. Our hearts have hardened and we have such strange ideas about God. The crowds today would more likely chase a saint out of town than ask his blessing. They do not tell us what we want to hear, they call us to repentance. This is not a message that many can bear today." She grew sombre and her eyes began to fill with tears. She wiped them with the back of her hand, "Lord have mercy," she whispered. We fell into silence and then she asked "When do you return to England?"

"On Wednesday," I said.

"You will have time to come and see us again then, before you go?"

"I would like that, thank you."

She got to her feet and gathered the cups from the table. As I stood the other nun came forward for a blessing and once more I knew I was standing before someone much closer to God than myself. I thanked them again and left them in the little room. In the church a handful of people were venerating the icons but it was quiet and still. I went into one of the side chapels and stood before the iconostasis for a while, thanking God for the encounter with the two nuns, and for all that I had heard. From one of the icons the image of a patriarch whose name I couldn't make out looked down at me with a mixture of fierce authority and gentle acceptance. My thoughts fell away and I stood with the saint for a few minutes, knowing I was with one who had been victorious in all the struggles I now faced. I asked for his prayers and left the monastery, emerging once more into the world of traffic and rush.

Chapter Ten

There are times when we know that there is great significance in the events and experiences of our lives. Outwardly there may be little to see, but as we grow older we learn to recognise when God is speaking to us. As I walked towards Red Square my heart was filled with the words of Mother D., and though I felt their immense presence, they brought a lightness to me. As I thought through some of the things she had said I realised there were many questions I wanted to ask, but I also knew that if I had asked them I would have prevented her from saying what she needed to give to me. I hoped for another opportunity to see her again before I left, and made a decision to write down as much as I could of what she had said when I got back to my room.

The towers of the Kremlin grew closer and it struck me as strange that the Soviets had allowed something so free spirited and unique like Saint Basil's Cathedral to exist alongside the walls of the place where the destruction of Christianity was plotted. There were fewer tourists at this time of day and I walked quickly through the square. At the opposite end from Saint Basil's, next to the imposing building of the State Museum, the bells of the Kazan Cathedral began to ring and I felt myself drawn towards them. It looks like a building slotted in amongst those around it, its orange and white arches in sharp contrast to the other darker buildings. Like Christ The Saviour Cathedral, this was another victim of the Soviets. The original building was torn down in 1936 in an attempt to secularise Red Square. The Kazan Cathedral gets its name from the wonderworking icon that is so familiar around the world. In 1612 Prince Dmitry Pozharsky was to face the armies of the Polish-Lithuanian Commonwealth to liberate Moscow. He prayed many times before The Lady of Kazan holy icon which was known to bring protection to whole cities. When he was victorious the prince built a small wooden church on the corner of Red Square dedicated to the Virgin of Kazan. This remained only until 1632 when it was lost to a fire, and Tsar Michael I had a new church built, but this time in stone. The church quickly became one of the most important in Russia, and not just because of its location. On the anniversary of the military victory it had been built to commemorate, the Patriarch and Tsar would lead a procession from the Kremlin to the church. As its importance grew, so did its physical shape, with so many additional towers and expansions that little of the original building is now identifiable.

Peter Baranovsky, the architect who worked on its renovations up to 1932, begged Stalin not to demolish it, but though his entreaties failed, he did manage to persuade the leader to spare Saint Basil's. Not long before the USSR was to collapse, a small chapel was permitted to be built on the site in 1990, and after Russia's liberation the reconstruction of the cathedral took place between 1990 and 1993. The original architectural measurements were used to produce as an exact copy as could be managed, which accounts for its refusal to merge into the more contemporary structures around it.

On the day of my visit there was a good crowd inside as I entered, and despite the polite notice asking for photographs not to be taken, tourists were waving their mobile 'phones around to capture the beauty of the arches and icons. Amongst all this there were Christians lighting candles and venerating the holy images, ignoring the worldly activities around them.

I approached the gilded iconostasis which glittered even in the dimly lit church. As I lit my first candle I saw the copy of the Kazan Icon (the original is in the Yelokhovo Cathedral, in the village of Yelokhovo, not far from Moscow). I had carried a laminated print of it in my wallet for a number of years, and to see it before me felt extraordinary. It didn't matter that this was a reproduction, I prayed before it expecting the same blessing as I would the original. This was the place where it had been placed, this was a church in which the Mother of God had been venerated for so many centuries. And as with any copy of her image, be it a print on laminated paper or a work of great art, through it she is able to reach out and help us. I welled up with a sweet feeling of joy which felt like a blessing through her prayers. The icon's very beginning had been miraculous when its location in a burned house had been revealed in a vision to a little girl. The icon had immediately been recognised as being a gift from the Mother of God. I was in awe to be in the presence of such a holy object, and once more I rejoiced at Christ's victory over all earthly powers; not least for the many martyrs whose temporal existence had been ended at Stalin's orders.

Eventually I left the cathedral, full of optimism and gratitude. The Kremlin walls loomed over me as I walked the length of Red Square, but I knew the power they represented was limited. I crossed the Moskva River and followed it back to Gorky Park. I was hungry and there was a small wooden coffee shop that I had walked by each day. Through the glass front I could see they had only one customer and decided to take advantage of the quiet. It was good to get in out of the cold and two young women at the counter greeted me with smiles. Neither spoke English, and when my attempt to explain in Russian that I wanted fasting food failed, I settled for a black coffee. As I nursed it for warmth and sipped it slowly, it was as satisfying as any meal. I watched skateboarders roll by, and ladies with their toddlers in pushchairs. There was an atmosphere of civility to it all; a world away from the gangs of youths that hang around in most London parks.

I began to think about making my confession the following morning. There was much I wanted to say, but none of the priests at the Pilgrim Centre spoke English. My Russian wasn't up to the job, but I couldn't face having a lay person translate my words. I remembered the phrase book I had brought with me and a plan of action began to form. I would write my confession out in English and use the little phrase book to translate as closely as I could what I needed to say. Once I had come up with the idea I was enthusiastic to try it out and quickly finished my drink.

What had seemed a simple idea turned out to be very frustrating. None of the phrases quite matched up enough to convey exactly what I needed to say. I began building elaborate combinations in an attempt to make my points clearer, but which only created complicated, rambling sentences that I suspected would sound ridiculous to a native speaker. I cut them down as much as I could and hoped the meaning was discernible. I wrote out the phonetic version of it all on two sides of A4 paper and began reading it aloud to practice the pronunciation. After ten minutes or so it started sounding like Russian to my ears, and I tried to tell myself the priest would understand: a little voice in my head, however, was insisting I would sound like an idiot. But I had no choice, this was the only way I could confess, and I couldn't attend another Divine Liturgy without receiving Holy Communion. I had known Russians who received only two or three times a year but continued to devoutly attend the Liturgy. It made me realise what great discipline it required, and also how painful it must be for them at times.

In the evening I received a message on my Kindle telling me the couple I was to meet were on their way. Outside it had begun to rain heavily and I imagined them out there trudging through the dark. About five minutes before they were due to arrive I went out to greet them and huddled next to the wall of the church to stay as dry as I could. But as the time passed there was no sign of them and I went back in to check for more messages. There was a second message asking me to confirm the address and name of the church as they had ended up in the wrong place. I sent them the details and a minute later they assured me they would be with me in ten minutes. I repeated my trip out to meet them and again they didn't show up. I went back to my room and asked them if everything was okay. They assured me they would arrive in the next five minutes. It was now more than an hour after our original meeting time, and I was becoming a little frustrated. Over the next few days I was to discover that my reaction revealed far more about me than it did anything about them.

A final time I stood trying to find shelter next to the church when A. and V. appeared at the church gate. He was carrying an umbrella which he held over her head. I waved with relief and in the dark I could see them smile.

"Father Spyridon," V. said, "we went to two churches." He struggled to find the words, and his accent was strong.

"Please, come inside. I'm so glad you made it." I led them up the steps into the kitchen where they removed their wet coats. Though better than my Russian, their English was very limited, and she had a large electronic tablet into which she typed everything she wanted to say. It translated her words into English, and after she typed she handed me the device to read. I made us tea and we slowly discussed the Pilgrim Centre. They asked about our mutual friend in England and were interested to know what I thought of Moscow. Eventually A. brought up their plan for the next few days, she was enthusiastic to act as a guide. V. worked in a museum outside Moscow, and they wanted me to catch the Metro out to the village where they would meet me and we would spend the afternoon together. And then on the following day, Monday, they would meet me in Red Square and give me a tour of the Kremlin. She had, until recently, been a tour guide there, and it was obvious how keen she was to have me learn all about it.

They both had the typical Russian broad cheeks, and also large expressive eyes. They dressed humbly but smartly, and though they were both a little younger than me, there was an air of maturity to them. I found myself warming to them very quickly.

They had come by Metro on a terrible night to meet me and they were going to give two whole days of their time. I should have felt nothing but gratitude, but the truth was I was harbouring very different thoughts. The prospect of travelling on the Metro to a town I didn't know was not something I wanted to do, and though they had gone out of their way to find me, the fact that they had been so late caused me to be unsure how far I could trust the plans we were making. Our inability to communicate very well only compounded my anxiety about it all, and I struggled to know what to do.

With everything agreed they set out into the cold to catch their train home, and I went back to my room. I spent some time trying to decipher the Metro timetable but I wasn't even sure which station I should start from. I looked at maps and weighed up my options, but the more I studied it all the more I felt a sense of panic. I began to imagine myself heading off to the wrong place, unable to get in touch with them, not even able to tell people where I wanted to get back to. In the face of their kindness I felt horrible doing it, but I sent a message trying to explain my doubts, and apologising for not being able to join them for the first day. It felt like an act of supreme ingratitude, but almost immediately they messaged me back brushing aside my apology and saying how much they still looked forward to meeting me in Red Square on Monday. A wave of relief passed over me. I put the Kindle away and took out my prayer book. There was now nothing to think about except preparing for the Divine Liturgy in the morning.

Chapter Eleven

The morning air was still cool as I made the short walk to the church. A single bell rang out to call us to the seven o'clock service and I was unsure how simplified the service would be at this time. Entering the church I found the area around the inside of the door crowded with people. I wasn't sure what was happening and decided to squeeze past them and use the lighting of my candles as an opportunity to see what was going on. The main iconostasis had just two candles flickering before it in the darkness, and no one was entering that part of the church. Immediately to my left there was a small side chapel, so small that the iconostasis had only one door to the north of the Royal Doors and nothing to the south. Between the people and the chapel three of the priests stood at stands holding icons, before which they were hearing confessions.

I lit my candles before the iconostasis and joined the waiting congregation who shuffled forward each time someone had finished their confession. Normally a priest confesses at the altar, but since I wasn't concelebrating I was happy to confess as the laity were doing. A young boy of about twelve was revealing his sins, and the priest bent forward to hear. Before the absolution he gave a detailed response to whatever the boy had said, and I thought of my own sons, and how grateful I had been to see them confessing at a similar age.

I had my script folded in my pocket, and nervously my hand gripped it out of sight. I felt the common anxiety so many feel in revealing their darkest secrets before a priest, but also I had the additional question of whether anything I had prepared really made sense. I had tried to address my feelings as I had prepared myself for the solemn rite, and I always brought to mind the words of Saint John Chrysostom who said "We rush to our sins but are ashamed when we repent. It should be the other way round." I believed these words, and held on to the fact that in a short while all the sins I was burdened with would be lifted from me; it always gave me courage to say whatever was shaming me. From my own experience from hearing confessions, I also knew that the priest would hold no judgement in his heart over whatever I revealed; in truth the astonishing courage and faith of people as they asked for God's forgiveness always leaves me in awe of their humility and trust. The understanding of God's Judgement and the eternal consequences to come, as well as His loving forgiveness in this life bring us back, again and again, to seek God's mercy. And the assurance of His forgiveness when we set our hearts on repentance brings a hope that nothing in the world can match.

Eventually I was ushered forward by one of the ladies standing next to me and I bowed beside the priest. The Russian words that had previously sounded so authentic now felt clumsy in my mouth. The priest remained impassive and I continued to read my list of sins. Whatever they conveyed to my fellow priest, I prayed that God would accept my attempt to fully disclose everything. When I reached the end I lowered my paper and bowed my head. It must have sounded more like his native tongue than I had feared because his response came in a long discourse on what I had told him, and he seemed to think I would understand his advice. I knelt before him and he placed his epitrachelion over my head. The sound of his deep voice repeating in Russian the words that I knew so well took all anxiety from me and I relaxed for a moment. As I stood we exchanged a kiss and I pushed the list of my sins deep into my pocket: they were gone.

I joined those who had made their confession, standing before the beautiful iconostasis. One of the priests had left the other two who continued hearing confessions and was censing the church. His purple vestments reminded us that we had entered the arena, it was the first Sunday of Lent. This Sunday is called the Sunday of the Triumph of Orthodoxy, when we give thanks for the victory of Orthodoxy over the iconoclasts, those who had tried to make the Church reject the holy icons. The Seventh Ecumenical Council declared that since Christ became a real human being, it is not only permitted, but it is necessary that we venerate Him through images of His incarnation. The whole physical universe has been changed by Christ becoming flesh. The things of the earth must be taken up to be used in worship: matter itself has become a means of the glorification of God. Saint John of Damascus defended the Church's position against the icon smashers, and all Christians were once more free to use icons to come closer to the saints and to God. I looked at the iconostasis, the rows of icons stood defending the truth of the incarnation, and declared the redemption of the whole cosmos.

At that moment I remembered that it was the anniversary of my ordination to the priesthood. A mixture of emotions welled up in me, and I had to make a conscious effort to hold back my tears. In 1988 when I had first encountered Orthodoxy, one of the major influences on my thinking had been Father Seraphim Rose. He had died six years before I discovered his writings, but his divinely inspired words had revealed to me something larger than the Christianity I had known up until that point. He never lived to witness the resurgence of Orthodoxy in Russia, and I knew that he was rejoicing in heaven to see what had happened. I have always tried to keep politics and issues of jurisdictions out of my faith, and so had never really engaged much with Father Seraphim belonging to the Russian Church Outside Russia. But now that I was priest in this jurisdiction, and that we were fully received under the Patriarchal shepherding of Moscow, I felt a great significance in being there on this important day.

The Sunday of the Triumph of Orthodoxy is the celebration of the true faith. The day when we declare through our veneration of the icons that Christ's incarnation means we who are created in the image and likeness of God may be restored to the Divine state. Through our repentance, our confession, our participation in the Body of Christ, we may be purified and made through grace to be like Christ. This is why I had made the trip to Russia. It was to find something beyond what my day to day existence could provide. Father Seraphim Rose often spoke of Holy Russia, and this phrase had taken root within me. The notion that a people and their culture could mysteriously reflect something of the Kingdom of God spoke to me. Just as the people of Israel had once been granted a special status in order to receive and protect the revelation of God, so now the Slavic people were standing in the face of a Godless world to proclaim the Christian faith. Russia's defence of traditional values and ethics was routinely mocked by western politicians and media, and the EU had declared the Russian Orthodox Church a threat to liberal values. This is not to suggest that every individual Russian is holy, but that collectively they had inherited the faith given to man by God, and were one of the few nations willing to protect it.

It is this that is the basis of the great cultural divide between East and West. Europe and North America now ride a wave of cultural change that is being orchestrated by those who reject Christianity.

In every aspect of western life, from sports to education and from politics to the way people dress, a spiritual rebellion is at work that tears their way of life from its Christian heritage. As a person raised within it, I was at least old enough to be able to recognise how alien modern western culture was to even the way of life I had known in my own childhood. But the extent to which my mind and heart were polluted by these false ideals and distorted morality, I could not be sure. Even just standing amongst Russian people was enough to make me aware of their comparative dignity, their stillness, and their embodiment of authentic Christian faith that is so quickly vanishing from the West. They were the living fruit born of centuries of struggle and even persecution: the martyrs had been raised up from amongst them even within living memory.

Russian culture expresses Christian faith in ways most westerners could not imagine. For example, even some of the days of the week take their names from Christian belief. Sunday is Voskresenie in Russian, which means resurrection, and Friday, Pyatnitsa comes from raspyat which is to crucify.

The choir was now standing close to us in the smaller chapel and they began to sing the hymns of the day. The litanies were prayed and we welcomed the holy gifts as they were carried in procession through the Royal Doors. I was aware of the elderly members of the congregation and the crucifixion they had endured under the communists. The reality of resurrection filled the church and was there in their humble faces.

When it came time to receive Holy Communion I joined the queue and approached the chalice. I was so overcome with it all that the priest had to ask me twice to speak my name. As soon as the Holy Mystery entered me I sensed the mystical connection between myself and those around me. And the union we shared extended beyond the walls of the Church, to the faithful across all Moscow, and around the world. But beyond our union, we were united with Christ. We stood with the whole host of Heaven, clothed in more than the angelic splendour, we were clothed in Christ Himself. In God's love for us we were raised above nature, beyond all things that are knowable through the earth: it is an unfathomable miracle that God can do this with such frail creatures as ourselves. Christ promised that those who eat His Body and drink His blood may have eternal life within them, and in that moment I understood how my salvation was entirely a matter of God's forgiveness.

I remained so absorbed in my thoughts that I was barely aware of how the Liturgy moved into a memorial service for the dead. The tone of the chants changed subtly and a small table of bread and oil was positioned to the side of the chapel. The priest swung the censor in a steady rhythm, and the whole congregation moved to pray with him. At the end he moved to before the royal doors and gave a sermon. Not a single member of the congregation left before he had finished, and as we eventually began to make our way out I could see the other priests making preparations at the main iconostasis for the later service.

I stepped out into the sunshine feeling completely at peace. I was about to head back to my room when the priest who had served the Liturgy appeared beside me with P..

"Father," he said through her, "would you like some breakfast?"

They had already shown me more kindness than I could have hoped for, but keen to speak to him I accepted his offer. On the little dining table the food was already laid out, a mixture of fruits, nuts, bread and a pasta dish. After the blessing P. spoke to him in Russian for a little while before he looked my way and seemed to act as though he had been neglecting me. As he said something P. turned to me and said "Father J. would like to discuss theology with you."

I felt my stomach tense a little, it was such a direct way of putting it and I suspected he was about to cross-examine me to ensure I was not harbouring any heretical beliefs. But I needn't have worried, his intention was friendly.

"England is a Protestant country," he said through P., "how did you become Orthodox?"

This was not the first time I had been asked this, and my impulse was often to simply say it was God's choice. But this time I understood his interest, especially on this particular day in the calendar.

"I was not raised Christian," I explained, "but I became Christian when I was about nineteen. A few years after that I met a monk from Mount Athos, he talked to me about prayer, and I realised I wanted to know more of what he was saying. I started reading as much as I could about Orthodoxy, this was before the internet so I had to order books from America. It took me a long time to realise I had to actually become Orthodox, that it wasn't enough to try and do Orthodox things outside the Church. I was serving as an Anglican minister, in the Church of England, and my conscience wouldn't let me avoid it any longer."

Father J. listened carefully as P. translated for him, he nodded at certain points and looked back and forth between the two of us. Immediately she finished speaking he said something and P. said, "Father J. wants to know if your wife was happy to become Orthodox."

"Yes," I said, "she was worshipping with some Russians who lived near us before I left the Church of England."

He was pleased to hear this and I didn't need P. to tell me that he kept saying "Good, good."

He pulled a quizzical face and said "Do you think the Protestants are Christian?"

I was surprised at this and said "I knew some very devout Anglicans, some of them were old enough to remember when the Church of England was different to how it is now. They had genuine, Christian hearts, if only they could have known Orthodoxy from their youth."

"He frowned at this and said "Forgive me for saying this Father, but I think you still retain a little of your old Protestant thinking. Of course there are devout Anglicans, there are devout people in every group, and even cults. There are devout Hindus, devout Muslims, but do you think such devotion will save them?"

"No," I said, "but I wouldn't equate any kind of devotion to Christ with devotion to these other things."

"No, please," his tone became less insistent, "I do not wish to suggest this. But personal devotion is only a part of what we need. If it was left to strength of feeling alone, Christ's message would have been very different. The West has made issues of faith an individual or personal matter. It has lost the necessity to belong to the Church, and an understanding of how the life of the Church shapes us. We are not saved alone but as part of Christ's Body. We cannot find salvation if we cut ourselves off from the vine. Christ warned us of this reality. No matter how much someone says they believe, if they are cut off, they do not have Christ's life within them, and it is only the life of Christ that saves us. It is God's grace, not the strength of our feelings."

"Yes," I agreed, "I accept that."

"And more than this, we must ask what it is they are devoted to. We cannot truly know God beyond the extent that He reveals Himself to us. The knowledge of God is found in the Holy Spirit, and we do not know the Holy Spirit unless He lives in us. Without the life within the Church we are devoted to nothing more than an idea of God, but it is not God Himself. Every human being is created with a spiritual need of God. This is why mankind's history is full of attempts to satisfy this need with different religions. Even men who do not know God need some way to express their spiritual yearning. It can be very profound, and even consume someone's life. But if it is nothing more than ideas which satisfy a part of this yearning, it does not bring salvation." He could see me thinking about this and said "I know this sounds harsh, but if we keep quiet and allow people to perish, allow them to die without Christ's life within them, how loving is that?"

I agreed with his sentiment and was about to explain something about the British sensibility, and our reluctance to say anything too confrontational when he said "Do you think they really believe in the Holy Trinity?"

I was caught off guard by the question and had to think a little. It wasn't something I had ever considered and before I answered I said "Why do you ask this?"

"I have seen some of their liturgical books, it is true that they mention Father, Son and Holy Spirit at the end of some prayers, but beyond this I cannot see how they worship the Holy Trinity. I have read just a little of their theology, and it makes me doubt them."

Still unsure how to answer I wanted more explanation for his enquiry. "Where do you think they are failing in this? Certainly they include the filioque in their creed, is this the reason you ask?"

He waved his hands in a gesture of acknowledgement, "The filioque is the foundation for many heresies. When the popes rejected the authentic faith of the Church a whole false theology was born. But the Anglicans have merged the three Holy Persons, they do not worship the distinct three hypostasis. Of course there is simple unity in God, but in everything He does and in every way that He reveals Himself to us, He is in three hypostases. We cannot know any one of the three Holy persons without the other two, but this does not mean they are merged into an indistinguishable solitary being. God's love is mysteriously expressed within Himself between the Three, this would be nonsense if He were not truly Holy Trinity."

"I don't think most Anglicans would disagree with you," I suggested, "but why do you think they believe something else?"

"God the Father is the source of all being, from Whom the Son is begotten. The Holy Spirit proceeds from the Father, not from the Father and the Son. Yes, they are equally uncreated, they share the same essence, but it is the Father Who is the origin of the Holy Trinity. Western theologians have permitted themselves to use their ideas to create doctrines about God that are not based in revelation. We cannot go beyond what God reveals of Himself, the mystery of God cannot be captured and defined by reason. Even Pope Leo III wouldn't say the heretical creed in Rome, he knew it went against the tradition of the Church, but he allowed it to be used elsewhere. Of course, they were at the beck and call of the Germans who were propping the popes up at this time, so they did as they were told."

I was in full agreement with everything he said, but still I could not see why he charged Anglicans with failing to worship the Holy Trinity. He had fallen into explaining to me problems with the filioque, but it hadn't answered my question. I tried again, "But what is it that makes you think Anglicans do not believe this, other than their acceptance of the filioque?"

"What experience is there of the Father? They make the Holy Scriptures the only means of knowing God. What kind of Christianity is this? If we are not united with God, how can we be changed by Him? Do we want to be like children, patted on the head and assured everything is alright now? Is that the goal? Of course not, we must struggle, we must be changed."

"Where do you see this expressed in Anglican worship?" I persisted.

"Anglicans reduce the Person of the Holy Spirit to a kind of effect, a relationship between the Father and the Son. They close their prayers with phrases that treat Him this way, as though He were not a full and equal Divine Person. This is terrible. It is the Holy Spirit Who makes us one with Christ, it is the Holy Spirit Who joins us to Him at baptism. If they lose the truth of who He is, how can they claim to know Him? If we believe wrong things about God, we cannot know Him. We are not called to live according to the letter of a law, or texts, but in the Holy Spirit. We do not use words like "valid" to describe our sacraments, this is not a court of law!"

He began to speak louder as his enthusiasm for the topic grew, and only when he caught P. glancing at me did he fall silent. He laughed a little at himself, "You see Father," he said, "I am too keen to get into a fight when it comes to defending our faith. There is a time and a place, forgive me."

I smiled back at him, "I am grateful for what you have said."

He seemed satisfied with this and returned to his food. When we had finished eating he told me he and one of the other priests were scheduled to visit a local care home that afternoon, and he apologised for having to rush off. Away from the theological issues his friendliness returned and I suspected he was a little embarrassed at having become so enthused. They returned to the church and I walked down to Gorky Park. There were a lot of people enjoying the sunshine and I found a bench near the river where I could sit quietly and reflect on the morning. I realised that Monday would probably be a return to being a tourist, which I didn't mind, but I wanted to visit the monastery one more time that weekend. I had a few hours before the evening service, so I stretched my legs out in the heat of the afternoon and watched the dark river rolling by.

Chapter Twelve

The Moscow streets now felt familiar and as I walked to the monastery I had no sense of being alien or even a visitor. On the path along the river two young men dressed in outlandish animal costumes were playfully trying to persuade two women to have their photographs taken with them. The women giggled at the attention and it was obvious that the men had their approach well-rehearsed. As they came past me I could detect the pleading in one of the men's voices and it was obvious a request for money was going to be the finale of their act.

I turned up towards the monastery and once more realised how little time I had left in Russia. Two more full days and then my mind would be turning to the return trip and figuring out how to reach the airport. But I pushed it all away, it was pulling me out of the moment, and stirring my anxiety. I would give P. a call at the Pilgrim Centre and see if she could help suggest a trustworthy taxi service. Once I had settled on a plan of action I brought myself back to where I was. I hoped to see Mother D. again and I had some questions prepared. So much of what she had said had been stirring within me and I knew I had to take the opportunity while I could. I had written many of her comments down and this had helped me to understand a little more clearly of what she had said, but there were still things I only later realised I needed clarifying.

I was a few minutes early and took the opportunity to venerate some of the relics in the side chapel. I stood quietly before an icon of Saint Martha, contemplating the things she had witnessed. Like so many saints who are mentioned in the life of Christ, her story was so human and ordinary and yet filled with miraculous events. I tried to let this realisation make me aware of how God is active and present in all our lives, however mundane they may feel to us.

I allowed myself to pray there a little longer than I should have, and by the time I joined the congregation the priest had already censed the church and was singing a litany. There were more nuns present than at any other of the other services I had attended, and the gentle way they sang the responses was very moving. I chanced a glance over at them and their attitude of prayer was displayed in everything about them: their bowed heads, their humble posture, the serenity in their faces. Like the paths my daily walks with my dog had carved into the Welsh hillside back home, concealed amongst the trees and rise of the hills, so the very presence of the nuns had been shaped by their lives of prayer. It was something beyond muscle memory or the effects of fasting, it was the moulding of their existence by the Holy Spirit. Just as I had recognised holiness in the monks on my visits to Mount Athos, so now I could see the very same grace at work in these women.

The young priest led us through the evening office, and the tone of his voice reflected the change in the liturgical atmosphere. The nuns sang back and forth across the church, verses and responses that beckoned all our hearts towards God. It was over too quickly and a hushed peace hung over us as we began to leave. Mother D. was already standing at the door to the little tea room and I was very relieved when she waved to me. Before I could reach her she disappeared inside and I wondered whether I had been invited over, and as I stood unsure what to do, another very old nun passed me and let herself in. As the door opened Mother D. beckoned me in from the table and I happily did as she wanted.

"How are you this evening father?" She stood and bowed to receive a blessing. The second nun did the same before taking a seat opposite me.

"I am well thank you." We exchanged a little small talk and she introduced the other sister: this time I made sure I caught the name. Mother L. spoke a little English, and she greeted me in a strong Russian accent with a weak voice.

"Mother D.," I said, "I have been thinking about some of the things you said last time I was here."

"Oh good," she smiled.

"A few questions came to me if I may ask them."

"Of course," she said, "let us assume that God has prompted these question in you. None of us knows how much God cares for us, or how much our

Guardian Angel suggests good things to us. So let us assume your questions must be asked."

"Thank you," I wondered if my questions would meet her expectations, but I agreed that it was important not to leave things unfinished. "You were talking about fear of God. I've struggled with reconciling this with our love for God. How can we fear and truly love God at the same time?"

"It is an important question," she nodded. "First we must understand that love, true love, is a victory over evil. When we love, we defeat the devil. The evil one wants us to hate as he hates, he wants us to cause and feel pain and separate us from God and each other. When we love we overcome this separation. But we are so sick with sin that without God it is not possible for any of us to love. To love with Divine love we must struggle to find and approach God. We cannot do this without repentance. Repentance draws us towards God because it is the abandoning of sin, turning away and rejecting evil. But being the creatures we are, we cannot begin to repent unless we fear the consequences of our sin. Fear of Judgement, fear of hell, this pushes us to repent. So you see, unless we first fear God we cannot ever truly love Him. True love of God is not acquired except through obedience and prayer. And we are not obedient unless we repent of our evil."

The second nun placed cups of hot sbiten before us and took her seat to listen carefully to Mother D.. "It is connected with what I said before," Mother D. continued. "Obedience and humility are the foundations of spiritual life. God sees our pride and helps us to be humble. He chastens us a little just like any good parent must guide their child. And even in good homes a child must fear their father's reaction if they are disobedient. Of course they know their father still loves them, but also that there are rules that must be obeyed for their own good."

I nodded my understanding, and said "How is it possible to reach a state of love for God but still fall away?"

Mother D. reacted quickly, "You assume that such love is the property of man. Not at all. If God abandons even the greatest saint they will fall and have no love. This is why we must struggle and suffer to reach the heights of spiritual perfection. Anyone who has truly drawn close to God knows full well the temptations and battles that have led to this condition. God permits us to endure these things so that we are made ready to hold on to what He gives us. It is not enough that we are obedient to Him outwardly. Obedience is not just a matter of behaviour, it must exist in the heart. In fact, no one can act in obedience unless his heart is obedient. This is why Our Lord warned us not just to avoid adultery, but not to allow even such desires inwardly. Obedience is a change of heart, it begins with repentance, which starts with fear of God. Do you see?"

The two nuns looked at me, there was a stillness in their demeanour that enabled me to feel comfortable in revealing what was troubling me.

"Forgive me," I said, "but can love and fear exist simultaneously in the same heart?"

Mother D. could see that my enquiry was not born of inquisitiveness and said, "There are two kinds of fear of God. You remember Holy King David tells us that the beginning of wisdom starts with fear of God. This is because where there is fear, there is obedience. The Church Fathers tell us that fear in the beginning gives birth to virtue, it prompts us to abandon the worldly pursuits that tempt us away from God. This is the first kind of fear. But the second is a higher kind. When we learn from obedience to hate evil, our hearts grow to yearn for all that is pure and holy. Obedience begins to bring joy, while sin brings us sorrow. A fear of falling into evil guards us, it guides us away from where temptation would lead us. The fear of losing God's grace, the fear of falling from fellowship with God like Adam did is pure, it is not fear of punishment, but is filled with love for God."

"I think I understand," I said, "so it is not strictly a fear of God, but a fear of losing His grace?"

"No, it is still fear of God," she insisted. "When a man reaches the heights of perfection he knows that he is still a sinner, still weak and capable of falling. This is why we must go through a lifetime of repentance to reach God. So that we retain the fear of God's withdrawal of grace. Only through repentance do we know the bitterness of our previous life, and so remain obedient through fear of falling into evil once more. It is not thinking of God's punishment so much as understanding that when we choose evil we reject God. When we turn away from Him we are no longer able to receive all that He wants to give us. It is our sin, the evil that we do that leads us to this condition. God's love is life, and when we reject love we reject life. Disobedience is the same as choosing death."

This final statement echoed what I had heard so many times before and at last I understood how she had brought me to link so many different ideas. "Thank you," I whispered, still absorbing her words, "I think I see."

Mother D. finished her drink and pushed her cup away from herself. She folded her hands in front of her and leaned slightly forward. "Is there anything else you wanted to talk about?"

I had read so many accounts of pilgrims visiting monks asking for a word on prayer, and despite my attempt on the previous visit, I clumsily said "Could you share a word on prayer with me?"

"What about, exactly?" She said.

I realised the question had not really come from my heart, in asking it I was only playing some imagined role. It was not a real question at all. Sensing my feelings Mother D. smiled again and said "You must understand, I am a simple nun. I am not well educated, and I have nothing special to mark me out from the other nuns. But if you ask something specific I might be able to repeat something I've heard from one of the wiser nuns."

I knew exactly what I needed to know. "Please could you tell me something about the Jesus Prayer, and also more about unwanted thoughts?"

As soon as I had said it I knew it was something my heart was asking.

She looked down at her dry hands, one finger rose and tapped on the knuckles of her other hand as she thought about my question. She looked up at me and said "Where to begin first. Do you mean unwanted thoughts in general?"

"No, distractions when we are praying. I still struggle with them."

She chuckled, "Still struggle! Do you think you will ever be entirely free from this struggle? Think about when you read a good book, or watch a movie, how your mind can be absorbed for hours. Such concentration! But then within thirty seconds of saying the Jesus Prayer you find your mind wandering. Do you see what is happening? The demons are happy for us to waste our time on entertainments, they do not bother us. But the moment we begin to pray they stir up every unnecessary thought and memory they can. The imagination is not a central part of our mind, and so the demons use it to create fantasies and ideas that will cause our emotions to get excited. It can be an obstacle to prayer even for those who have been in monasteries for many years. There are Holy Fathers who describe the imagination as like a bridge over which the demons pass into our soul. The only way to protect ourselves is to use the imagination in a holy way. When we allow the mind to recall our sins, our failings, when we ponder Christ's promises, the chaos of demonic imagination is overcome. This is the secret, to build structure and order so that the mind doesn't run this way and that. The demons will happily lead our imagination everywhere it pleases to go, but all the time their intent is to harm us. In the beginning it is good for us to use our imagination in this way. But as we advance, even this must be abandoned. There is a pure form of prayer that can only be achieved when all imagination is rejected, when we become absorbed entirely by God. Imagination will always bring to mind sensory objects and experiences. It stirs emotion through the memory of these and can provoke passions. And so we must train ourselves to cut off all outward memory, so that the world and its pull on us does not separate us from God. The mind can only be illuminated when it is not darkened by worldly thoughts. Christ dwells in pure hearts, He makes His home within us. How can we expect the Holy God to make His dwelling where there is pollution and earthly desires? The Fathers say a pure mind is the throne of God. This is because God dwells in and is known by those who have purified themselves not just of evil, but of all worldly concerns. Purity of mind is the single focus on God. This is where true prayer is found."

I felt my mind struggling to contain everything she was saying, it was beyond anything I had experienced in my own prayers. I recognised themes I had read about, but I understood that she was not just repeating what she had read, but was relating her own experience. As she spoke there was a certainty in her voice; this was not some academic treaty she was setting forth, but the honest reality of her own inner life.

"We must guard against images in our minds when we pray," she continued. "I remember a young English girl who told me that when she prayed she saw the image of Jesus in her mind as He was played in a film of His life. So she was praying to the image of an actor, not to God." Mother D. looked at the other nun who shook her head at this. Mother D. said "Thought and imagination are entirely different things. They come from different places: thought comes from the mind, but imagination is born of the passions. How can we pray to God if we are imagining things? The mind is not capable of imagining God, and so anything we imagine when we pray will prevent us from truly worshipping Him. If we imagine God then it is not God." She paused and in a low voice said "It is idolatry."

I suddenly remembered a time at University when my wife had spoken to a Franciscan nun for advice about prayer. The nun had told her to sit in front of an empty chair and imagine Christ sitting there, and speak to Him. Even being young and inexperienced in such things, we had recognised something dangerous in this, and only now did I fully see how God had protected us from such misguided advice.

For the first time the other nun spoke, her throat was dry and her accent made it difficult to follow everything she said. But a phrase stood out as she tapped her temple with her finger, "The mind must be deaf and dumb when we pray. Let nothing distract us from our Lord. When we are filled with thoughts of God, we do not want anything more. Say His name, say "Jesus", the demons cannot have us if we have His name with us."

Mother D. looked at me and said "You wanted to ask about this?"

"Yes," I said, "about the Jesus Prayer."

"That's right," the other nun said, "The Jesus Prayer." She crossed herself and her lips began to silently mouth the words as she prayed.

"Can you tell me something about how to say it more effectively? I asked.

"Effectively?" Repeated Mother D., "I'm not sure what you mean exactly. I cannot say much about the effect of the prayer, I am only a beginner, but I can tell you what I have been taught. When we say the Jesus Prayer it subdues the passions and puts fear into the demons. Many saints have told us that the name of Jesus burns the demons, it is a powerful weapon in our battle. If we learn to live with the prayer always, it enters into our soul and quietens the demands of our sinfulness. Christ comes to us, the Holy Spirit unites Himself to us; through the prayer we have a way of ignoring everything but God. This is what the Fathers call mental sobriety. When our Lord warns us of the dangers of drunkenness, it is not just wine that He is talking about. There is a drunkenness of the mind that is the chaos of the imagination. Stillness is necessary if we are to stay sober. We need prayer to live. We all know how the body dies if it doesn't breathe, so too the soul dies without prayer. Both give off the smell of decay when they die, but not everyone can recognise the stench of a dead soul. It is there in our disobedience, in our way of life, a dead soul is discerned in a life of passions and godlessness. This is the stench we see filling our world. When we pray we are doing what the angels do, when we live selfishly we do what the beasts do. We must strive to join ourselves with the angels, such prayer feeds us far more than any food feeds the belly. It is prayer that makes us into the temples of God, we were created for this from the very beginning. Without prayer we act against our very purpose, and we only have to look at the world around us to see the suffering and confusion that this brings. Think of this Father, the whole universe cannot contain God, but when we pray He lives within us. This is His love for us, it is a sign of the dignity with which all men were made. We may contain within us the One who cannot be contained."

My heart was soaring with her words, but still I knew I needed more practical advice and I had to take the opportunity to ask. "Please Mother D., can you tell me how to pray the Jesus Prayer."

"We must focus our whole mind on the words, let their meaning penetrate us. As we have said, shut out all distractions, and as the breath enters us so our attention should go down into the heart. If we are able to hold our self there with the prayer, we find it changes us, God's presence within us transforms us. But we must be patient. God sees the degree of our yearning for Him. Sometimes the demons will tell us we are bored, that we are hungry, that our sick friend needs visiting. But whatever comes, good or bad, ignore it all and by force of will stay with Christ."

I knew I was only just setting out on the journey and Mother D. was inviting me forwards from a point on the distant horizon. I had little hope of ever reaching such heights of prayer and said "So much of this is beyond me. I don't mean I could never do this, but where I am now is far from what you describe."

"You are not a monk," she said matter-of-factly, "and even for us these are things we are yet to fully know. But we must not lose hope. Experience teaches us patience, and from patience we learn to hope in God. When we are tempted we must know that God is testing our faith, He is teaching us patience. It is a blessed state when we endure temptations, and God does not permit us to be tempted beyond our strength. We must set our eyes on the Heavenly joys, knowing that they are infinitely greater than the earthly struggles we endure now. Christian love for our Lord is demonstrated in the way we endure afflictions, and in the way we wait patiently on Him. We must rejoice in our suffering, it will bring a mysterious joy to our hearts. Whatever stage of life we find ourselves in, trust in God always, let hope blossom within us. But above all, learn patience. Prayer is like a ladder, and we must climb on every rung to reach the top. It is no good becoming impatient and reaching too high, too soon. But we must also beware, even when we feel our hands gripping the rung on the top of the ladder, we can still lose our grip and fall. And what a fall it is from such a height. Each rung consist of different things; psalmody, silence; all the things necessary to acquire prayer. But common to each is humility, there is no true prayer without humility, whether we are beginners or saints."

"What is the most important thing to do to achieve humility?" I said.

"Saint Anthony taught people that we must repent of our sins and expect temptations until the day we die. He said that the only way to become humble through this is self-reproach. It is such a simple thing," she said, "and yet it brings so much. If we reproach ourselves then we are untouched by slander, we accept all struggles as befitting our sinfulness, and we understand that our just reward is hell. Seeing this fills us with gratitude to God, we recognise how merciful and compassionate He is, and hope in His mercy gives us strength."

The other nun touched Mother D.'s arm and spoke in Russian, and for a moment they confirmed something with one another. Mother D. turned back to me and said "But we must be careful. Even when the Holy Spirit brings us comfort, the demons try to mislead us. When we are tired, when we have struggled and begin to rest, we can feel a false comfort that brings a sweetness or a sense memory of something from the world, or even carnal feelings. The remembrance of Christ's name will help discern such tricks, the Jesus prayer instils sobriety enough to resist these false comforts."

"Is this a kind of prelest?" I asked.

"Yes, certainly," said Mother D., "but prelest is more than this. When we talked about imagination, I was talking about prelest. It is important that when we pray, all images must be rejected, so that even if we were to see an angel or our Lord's face before us, we must not accept it. When we understand our sinfulness we know how unworthy we are of such visitations, and the demons are simply trying to provoke pride in us or perhaps looking for a way to mislead us completely. This is why I worry for men who have received high educations in the world. It is very difficult for us when we have learned great knowledge to understand that our learning is merely the repetition of facts, or the application of facts in innovative ways. The Church Fathers warn us that no man who considers himself wise will ever enter the mysteries of God. We may learn many things externally, but only when we see the foolishness of our own hearts can we begin to learn from God. The wisdom of the world is distorted, it is foolishness before God; it gathers from the earth but rejects eternity."

"It may seem a silly question," I said, "but how do we recognise this kind of humility in ourselves. Is it possible to see it and not become proud?"

"We know we are still proud when we see our self-reliance, when we trust our own opinions, when we feel confidence in ourselves before God.

134

When we feel anger at insults, or insist on being heard, then we know the demons tricked us into filling our heart with arrogance. God does not turn away from us even in such a condition. He permits us to fall, to be tempted, He allows us to suffer the consequences of our pride so that we may be humbled. There is an old saying that says if we don't want God to humble us, we had better learn humility. Do you see how God works? Even demonic temptations can become a means of virtue. If our enemies stir up blasphemy and all kinds of evil passions within us, let these lead us to humility when we see them. So long as we judge ourselves, we will remain acceptable to God."

She looked down at her hands again, and the air around us was charged with an intense focus, a realisation that I had to hold on to everything she was sharing. Eventually she looked up and said "It's getting late Father, but before you go there is one more thing I need to say. So many people become distracted by the wrong things in their spiritual lives. They read a few lines from the life of a great ascetic and become obsessed with the outward aspects of how the saint lived. I have met people fixated with not sleeping in a soft bed, or refusing to use a pillow. These little distractions that become important to them. This is how the demons work. They make us focus on what is not important, and what will not save us. We must always watch our hearts and discern the passions there. Our work is to pull out anger, irritability, judgement of others, pull out the corruption that distorts Christ's image within us. We can become exhausted fussing over inconsequential things and not have the strength to work on what is crucial. It is better to lie on a soft, fluffy bed if we repent of our sins, than to be so strict about our physical circumstances that we become proud of our efforts. Let us do what is necessary before we try to go beyond it. One rung of the ladder at a time, and each in order."

She reached into her pocket and handed me a small laminated picture of Saint Martha. "Take this with you, Father, and remember the miracles she witnessed while living an ordinary life."

She glanced at the watch on her wrist and stood up, "Your blessing, Father."

I thanked them for their time once more and after venerating an icon of the Mother of God near the door, left the monastery. It was dark and very cold outside. The streets were quiet and I hurried back pulling my rassa tight around me. The lights of Moscow across the river were beautiful, but my eyes remained fixed on the floor before me. I couldn't bear for anything to distract me from the words of the Jesus Prayer.

Chapter Thirteen

I arrived at Saint Basil's Cathedral ten minutes before I was due to meet A. and V. and already there were many tourists strolling through Red Square. Feeling a little self-conscious standing where I was, I took a walk to the far end of the square, constantly glancing up at the red walls of the Kremlin. By the time I had made it back my new friends were waiting there and they reacted with big smiles when they saw me. I was relieved at this as I wasn't sure how they might have felt about my cancellation of our other excursion.

Once we had shared our greetings A. raised her electronic tablet and said "It is much easier now, look." Instead of having to type everything out they had downloaded some software that translated speech directly. She lifted it to her face and in a computerised voice it said "We will begin our tour now, Father." As someone old enough to remember a world without computers, this felt very futuristic to me, and standing next to an ancient cathedral struck me as an odd place to first encounter such technology.

Immediately in front of the cathedral is a bronze statue of Prince Dmitry Pozharsky and Kuzma Minin who gathered an army of volunteer soldiers to expel the Polish-Lithuanian invaders in the early 1600s. The statue itself only dates back to 1812 but the weathered bronze gives it the impression of being much older. It was another reminder of how Russia's history has been one of invasions and patriotic efforts to protect the homeland and how the Russian people continue to honour the sacrifices of the past.

"We will now see the oldest monument in Red Square," the computer translated. They led me just a few paces away from Saint Basil's to a stone structure that I hadn't paid any attention to before. It was little more than the remains of an outer wall, and as we climbed the half dozen or so steps up to it A. spoke quickly in Russian into her tablet. It was another remnant from a history that had helped preserve the nation, but I must admit I paid little attention to the details.

We walked beneath the imposing red wall of the Kremlin, and I mentioned the Christians who had been interrogated and tortured within. V. grew very serious, his brow furrowed and he said, "We still live with this reality."

I was unsure what he meant and said, "You mean the memory of how the Soviet's treated you?"

"Yes, of course, but more, beyond this. Even today we know what governments can do to us. Tomorrow is not certain. Today we have peace, thanks be to God, but tomorrow…who knows?"

"I have read a lot about how President Putin has supported the Church," I said, "do you think this will only be for a short time?"

"Who knows?" He shook his head. "Governments do not always show us what they are doing."

"But President Putin is a real Christian isn't he? His faith seems genuine."

"Yes, yes," V. said. "I think he is a good man, a good leader."

"And the Church has benefited from closer ties with the government?" I asked.

"There are many churches being built all over Russia. This is a good thing. But…how can I say this. The Church and the government exist for different reasons. One is to help us reach the heavenly kingdom, the other must deal with the politics of this world. With such different purposes, I do not think it is ever good for the Church and the government to be so close. This is only my opinion, many Russians disagree with me. But I was not so young when our government was taking priests away to labour camps. Monasteries were closed and monks arrested. We must never forget what governments can do, even if right now we have a Christian president. Do you understand my point?"

I assured him that I did, and seeing the pain in his eyes as he remembered the events of the recent past struck me hard as we walked with such freedom in modern Moscow. As we reached the museum at the far end of the square they led me through a large archway to a smaller but more modern square that was surrounded by high buildings that were decorated with intricate lighting. The large glass front of a shopping area was to our right as we followed the Kremlin wall to the left. Ahead of us two soldiers stood to attention either side of a flickering fire. This was the Eternal Flame commemorating the fallen of the Second World War. Many millions of Russian soldiers had remained unaccounted for when the war ended, and since 2014 a day of remembrance has been celebrated with solemn services held here at the tomb of the Unknown Soldier. Russia lost more of its people in the war than any other country, perhaps twenty-seven million, half of whom were civilians.

As we approached I looked at the young soldier standing rigid in his heavy uniform, his AK47 at his shoulder. A. looked at her watch and told me we should wait to watch the changing of the guard which happens every hour. As we stood before the flame A. said, "The Germans made it as far as Zelenograd in 1941, many people were killed. The remains of the soldier were brought here in 1966, the Communists tried to claim the victory as part of their own political victory, but the Russian people have always known that the defence of Russia has been to the glory of God."

We stood in silence for a little while, the Statue of the Russian helmet beside the flame was very moving, and there was a hushed attitude of respect amongst the people around us. The stillness was interrupted by the crunch of military boots on the pavement as a group of eight soldiers suddenly appeared from one of the gateways in the wall and marched towards us. They marched quickly, and there was a tremendous power in their movement. The practiced choreography of replacing the men at their station was flawless, and the two men who had been baking in the sunshine were escorted back into the Kremlin.

We followed their route and went down through Alexander Garden to the tourist entrance of the Kremlin. It was a large glass structure that protruded out from the red wall, and we joined the short queue waiting outside. Despite the posters and the atmosphere of any tourist attraction, this was an entrance to the Kremlin itself, and the security was tight. Armed guards stood either side of an airport-style metal detector, and as we entered something in my pockets set off the alarm. A young woman officer approached me and instructed me to empty my possessions into a box. Once more I stepped through and the alarm rang again. She swept a hand-held device over me and decided I wasn't a threat. All the time one of the armed soldiers watched us carefully, and it was a relief to be waved on.

At one of the counters we paid for our tickets and V. asked about something. The man at the desk pointed to a door at the back of the room and A. and V. led me over to it. I had no idea what was happening. Inside was a small room which resembled a bank, with five women sitting behind glass panels. Once more V. spoke in Russian and as he looked back at me as he spoke I realised I was the subject of conversation. He turned to me and said, "Do you have any identification with you?"

The question took me by surprise, "Why, is there a problem?"

"No," he assured me, "do you have anything with you?"

"Only my passport," I said.

The woman behind the counter said in English "Your passport will be fine." I was uneasy handing it over, and my uncertainty was accentuated when V. told me to give the woman just over a hundred roubles. As I slid the money through the slot at the bottom of the screen she pushed an electronic device back to me. With it came a booklet of instructions: it was an audio tour guide.

"This will make it easier," V. said.

We followed the arrows though a narrow hallway and emerged in the Kremlin grounds. It is a large complex of buildings set in spacious grounds. In perfectly Received Pronunciation the voice from my tour device told me that the name "Kremlin" means nothing more than a fortified castle, and that this is the largest active palace in the whole of Europe. The voice instructed me to look up at the giant red stars that sit on the top of the towers. These images of communism were placed there in 1935 I learned, being made of the melted double headed eagles that once proclaimed Russia's Orthodox identity.

As we walked between the manicured lawns V. pointed to the golden onion domes that peeked from behind the other buildings, and though he said nothing, I nodded. This was once a small town in itself, back in the 1100s, from which the suburbs of modern Moscow slowly grew. It wasn't until the 1300s that the centre of Russian political power was based in the Kremlin, and through the centuries many invading armies have recognised its symbolic importance. Napoleon ordered it to be destroyed during his brief occupation of the city, but the same winter weather that helped force his armies back also prevented his demolition experts from carrying out their work.

The Kremlin is roughly triangular shaped, its walls enclosing sixty-eight acres of land. I was surprised at just how large it was, and the variety of buildings was also unexpected. There are still four cathedrals and five separate palaces on the grounds, something which points to a history stretching way beyond Soviet rule. Before we entered any of the buildings we came to the largest bell in the world. The Tsar Bell broke before it could ever be rung, and now sits on a slightly raised pedestal. We took our turn amongst the other tourists having photographs beside it, and despite it never having been heard, its sheer size proclaims the great intention behind it.

A short walk from the bell and we came to another monument to building things big: the largest canon in the world. Cast from bronze in 1586, historians argue over whether it has ever been fired, but as a symbol of Russian military power it is still effective today. Much like the missiles processed through Red Square, this was intended to convince the Russian people of their own security, but also to remind potential invaders that any attack on Russia would be costly.

To the right of the path was a grand looking building that V. pointed out, "That is Putin's palace."

"Does he actually live there?" I asked.

"Only sometimes, listen to the tour guide."

I looked up the number on my guide map and pressed the button on the device. I was informed that that the Grand Kremlin Palace was built in 1839 as an attempt by the Tsar to equal the splendour of St. Petersburg's Winter Palace. The fact that it was still standing revealed how the Communist leaders had managed to incorporate so much of the reviled royal luxuries into their own lifestyle. We turned off the path and entered Cathedral Square which is enclosed by stunning white buildings. I came to an involuntary stop as I tried to take in the reality around me. Any one of these buildings would be an astonishing sight, but to be surrounded by them was extraordinary. I exchanged glances with my Russian friends, and without needing to say anything we knew we were all experiencing the same sense of wonder.

V. pointed to the cathedral that stood slightly apart from the others and as we approached it our sense of its height above us made us tilt our heads back as we walked. The single golden dome shimmered in the bright sunlight, and this ancient structure embodied to me the truth of Russian history more than anything I had seen. The Church of the Deposition of the Robe of the Holy Virgin is smaller than the other cathedrals around it, but its simplicity and elegance equals any of them. It was the site of a church built as early as the mid-fifteenth century when the people of Moscow offered their thanks to God for their deliverance from a Tatar invasion; it struck me once more how so many of the monuments and churches were linked to Russia's struggle to survive in the face of hostile invaders. Metropolitan Jonah of Moscow chose this church as the private temple of worship for himself, and this tradition continued with the Patriarchs that followed. The Soviets prevented services until 1933, and today the Patriarch of Moscow serves a Divine Liturgy there just once each year on the feast of the Deposition of the Robe (15th July).

As we entered my senses were overloaded with the frescoes and statues which filled every available space in the cube-shaped interior. Saints looked down at us from the walls, their ancient colours still vibrant, as though filled with divine light, though they were painted in 1644. The dome above us was supported by four ornate pillars, and we gazed in awe, trying to absorb the images: it seemed the whole host of Heaven was present with us. We moved to the iconostasis where two enormous silver candle stands held finely decorated candles. The Royal Doors date back to 1627, and above them stood many rows of saints that reached up to the ceiling. Every Orthodox church is capable of opening our hearts to God's presence, but praying in one so ancient, where divine services have been offered by so many saintly patriarchs, is a profound experience.

V. indicated that I should follow him through to another room where glass cases housed over eighty statues and wood carvings. I had not seen this style of iconography before, they were carved into dark wood in a style unique to Russia. Many of them carried signs of having been attacked by those who desecrated the churches, and to see their survival in the face of such unholy violence communicated a great reassurance. A large carving of the Mother of God from the seventeenth century looked like it could have been painted only yesterday, its colours hadn't faded and the face of the Mother of God looked out with as much tenderness and concern for us as any icon I had seen. At first it felt strange to venerate an icon shielded behind a glass panel, this area was more museum than temple, but the images could not be treated like a secular exhibition, and with the room empty of tourists I bowed and kissed the glass.

Outside once more V. and A. led me towards the Annunciation Cathedral. As we approached we marvelled at the eight golden domes surrounding the central dome above them. Built to connect with the Grand Kremlin Palace, it projects a degree of splendour that I had never known before. It was the personal chapel of the Tsars and was built in the 1480s. Grand Duke Ivan III had the cathedral built where churches had stood for the previous two hundred years, and many of the icons that came from the earlier temples were used in the new cathedral. It was Ivan III who had a private staircase built from his chambers into the cathedral, but when a fire caused damage to the temple in 1547, it was Ivan the Terrible who had paid for its restoration and the addition of more domes. The cathedral was used for all royal baptisms and weddings, even when the Tsars relocated to St Petersburg, and this royal link maintained its importance within the national identity of Russia. Through the centuries the Polish, Lithuanian and French invaders ransacked the cathedral, not only stealing its treasures but abusing its interior. The cathedral was restored again in the early 1800s until another fire damaged it during the Russian Revolution, and once in power the Bolsheviks closed it down and it was turned into a museum. The Communists believed that by declaring the Christian faith a matter of historic curiosity they could eradicate it from the people's hearts: they were wrong.

Unlike the other cathedrals in the Kremlin, which show evidence of foreign influence in their design, The Annunciation Cathedral is more typically Russian, and as we came closer we could see the ornate patterns along the edge of the roof that stood out from the pristine white limestone walls. The doorway is imposing in many ways. When they built the cathedral over the remnants of the previous temple, it meant incorporating a doorway that is five or six times the height of any normal entrance. Also the doors themselves were cast in bronze and are covered in gold foil.

Inside we passed through a small gallery to the main church. Immediately we were confronted with the large sixteenth century iconostasis that has the look of something very ancient. Though it is full of icons, it maintains a simplicity in the way they are arranged, and I became aware of myself as someone from a much later time period, almost as if I had travelled through the centuries. Once more the walls were covered in beautiful frescoes which followed the curve of the walls up to the dome where Christ looked down on us. The windows around the base of the dome allowed light to pour in around His icon so that He was surrounded in light.

Moving from church to church in such close proximity meant a deliberate effort was needed to prevent ourselves entering a tourist state of mind. As we wandered through the side chapels the impact of the colours and sheer number of icons made it easy to succumb to an almost worldly appreciation of them rather than approach them as holy objects. I struggled with these feelings, and when I took some photographs I knew how far I was drifting from where I wanted to be. I decided to remove the headphones of the guide device and try to encounter the icons in the way they were intended, rather than with historical facts flooding my mind.

Once outside we headed towards the Dormition Cathedral, sometimes know to westerners as the Cathedral of the Assumption. Ivan III saw construction begin in 1475 and it took another four years to finish. As we approached the arched entrance V. said "This is the mother church for all Russia."

At first I was unsure what to make of the statement. In many ways its exterior was simpler than the other cathedrals, looking more box-like with less adornments. Its white walls weren't as clean as those of the other cathedrals which added to its appearance of great age. The five golden domes, representing Christ and the four evangelists, became the model for many churches across Russia. But as we entered I began to understand its importance beyond any historic links. Surrounded by the now familiar walls of frescoes, the body of the church was filled with small crypts. They sat dark and sombre, and my Russian wasn't good enough to read the inscriptions. "What are these?" I asked V..

"These are the tombs of Moscow's Metropolitans and Patriarchs," he said.

I stood gazing at their arrangement, it looked haphazard, and yet each was carefully positioned with a respectful distance from any other. Seeing the expression in my face V. said, "The Bolsheviks allowed one last Divine Liturgy to be served here at Pascha in 1918, and then even this cathedral was closed. Many of its treasures were sold by Lenin and they still sit in other churches around the world."

The next Christian service was not held there until 1990, and once the Soviet regime collapsed the cathedral was returned to the Church in 1992. Such recent oppression of the Church had become another part of Russian history, but for now those who had endured it were still alive.

We made our way to the iconostasis which seemed even bigger than all we had seen so far. It was built in 1547 but in 1626 the first of additional sections was added to increase its height. V. leaned close to me and said, "When the old Tsars conquered cities, they would select the best icons and bring them here. I am not sure this is a good thing but it is very impressive."

I understood his feelings, but seeing the collection gathered together made me wonder at how God can create something so beautiful out of questionable human activity. We spent some time slowly studying the biblical scenes depicted in the frescoes, and seeing such familiar moments from the life of Christ made me aware of how the people who had worshipped here five hundred years before had expressed the same faith as us, and had hoped in Christ just as the Church had taught us to do today.

Outside we stood admiring the cathedral domes and V. said, "There was a medieval burial site here, Christians have worshiped here since at least the twelfth century, perhaps earlier."

Such long periods of time were filled with people struggling with the same fears and human longings that fill all of our hearts. "We are not really any different to the people who built it," I said.

"We have lost so much," said Ivan, "but still God offers us everything we need."

He met me with a steady gaze and then added, "It is not so long ago, even within my memory, you would not have been able to stand here dressed like that without a rifle at your back." Before I could respond he turned and A. and I followed him across the square towards a wooden door leading to the Patriarch's Palace. Built in the mid-1600s under the direction of Patriarch Nikon, it was the meeting place of the Holy Synod but today functions as a museum. It contains a mixture of vestments and various religious objects associated with different Patriarchs, which may suggest it is of little more than historical interest, but this is far from true. The holy objects now displayed behind glass still retain their link with the services they were used in, and like any relic that links us to the saints, being close to them stirred an awareness of the thin veil that separates us from the heroes of our faith who now live with Christ.

The main chamber was where the chrism oil for all of Russia was made. Two huge vats presented to the Patriarch by members of the British royal family still sit there. The heating pipes are still connected to the circular bowls that stretch ten feet in diameter and are nearly five feet in height. It is easy to imagine the Patriarch praying over the mixture of oils as priests and deacons stirred the warm liquid. The large capacity was a reminder of the great quantity of chrism oil that was needed to serve the countless churches across the Russian cities, towns and countryside.

V. and A. led me through to a series of smaller rooms where items connected to the royal family are preserved. There were displays of embroidery that the martyred girls had worked on, and seeing the individual stitches that the princesses had concentrated on was very moving. There were also items of furniture from their bedrooms, wardrobes and dressing tables. Such ordinary pieces of wood reminding us of the reality of their family life away from public duties.

We went down into the Twelve Apostles Church where a seventeenth century wooden iconostasis still stands. The fine carving was another example of distinctly Russian sensibility, its figures and overall design looking like nothing that could be found in any other country. There was also a display showing the development of iconography through the centuries, some of the earlier examples reminded me of Ethiopian iconography, and it was clear from the icons that up until the seventeenth century Russian taste had remained little affected by western sensibility.

There were signs instructing visitors not to take photographs, and even with a stern looking lady watching from a small desk, everyone snapped away. I turned from some icons and discovered A. had been photographing me looking at them. I felt a little uneasy to be breaking the rules but A. smiled when I caught her and I realised not all regulations in Moscow are as strictly adhered to as others.

Outside once more we followed the footpath down along the inside of the Kremlin wall and V. explained that my ticket permitted me entrance to the Kremlin armoury but theirs did not. I wasn't particularly interested in seeing it, but since I had paid for the ticket and not wanting to offend my guides, I left them outside and went into the museum. I was quickly glad I had, far from being an exhibition of weaponry, there were cases filled with all kinds of silverware, suits of armour, and many royal robes worn at coronations. Some of the armour dates back to the twelfth century, and I could imagine how terrifying it must have been to face men dressed this way in battle. I could easily have spent a long time in there, but I didn't want to leave V. and A. waiting and so I made my way round the exhibits at a brisk pace. When I emerged back into the daylight, V. was particularly keen to know my response and I could see his sense of pride over his nation's history.

The footpath took us past the official entrance to President Putin's residence, and there were many soldiers standing around nursing their machine guns. These were not the cheap knock-off AK47s sold to militias all over the world, they were impressive looking weapons.

Back at the museum entrance I reclaimed my passport and V. and A. began walking toward the Metro. It was now early evening and large numbers of people were pouring out as they returned from work. I stepped beside V. and said "Where are we headed?"

V. moved out of the way to one side to let the crowds pass us and said "We will catch the Metro, you can come with us, we would like to buy you dinner."

I knew that if I took a Metro ride I would have difficulty getting back and said "No, you've been so generous with your time, let me buy you a meal to say thank you."

The words got confused in translation and it seemed as though they thought I didn't want to eat with them. I tried again to explain that I would like to buy them some food, but very humbly they accepted what they thought I was saying and began to say goodbye.

Before we parted I said, "On Wednesday I must go to the airport. If I send you a message, do you think you could help me figure out which Metro train to catch?"

"Of course, we will help you," V. said, and after shaking my hand they turned and disappeared into the Metro crowd. I walked back to Red Square which was no longer busy, and as the sun began to set I took some photographs of Saint Basil's Cathedral bathed in the orange glow of the evening light. Crossing the Moskva River I stopped and watched the water flowing beneath me. V. and A. had reinforced my impression of Russians as Kind and hospitable, but at this point I had no idea just how kind they would be.

Chapter Fourteen

After the Divine Liturgy at the monastery, Mother D. signalled that I should follow her. On the little table where we sat for tea was a map and a small notebook.

"Please, Father," she said, "take a seat. There is something I want to ask you."

As I pulled one of the chairs out from under the table she turned her back to me to fill the kettle. From the shape of the river I immediately recognised the city on the map as Moscow, and I quickly spotted some of the places I had visited. I was curious as to why she should want me to see it.

Mother D. turned and caught me studying it, "There is somewhere I think you should visit, Father."

I received this news with a little trepidation, my lack of confidence with the Metro system meant risking a taxi ride. She placed a cup in front of me and said "Last night when I was praying, I had a strong feeling that you should visit Saint Tikhon before you return to England."

I wasn't sure how to react, I began to mouth an answer but nothing came out. Mother D. chuckled, "This has come as a surprise to you?"

"Yes, I have to go to the airport tomorrow night, will I have time to make the trip?"

She shook her head, "It isn't a trip, Saint Tikhon's relics are here in Moscow. If you catch the Metro to Shabolovskaya, you can visit Donskoy Monastery. I know a priest there who will talk to you. He speaks good English, I will email him and arrange it." Her amusement at my reaction continued.

I wanted to get out of it, my timidity was telling me to spend my last two days visiting the same churches I had already been to. But while my instinct was to play it safe, something in me told me I shouldn't ignore the offer. "When were you thinking?" I asked.

"I will contact him before lunch and you can visit tomorrow morning. His name is Father M., I am sure he will have far more to say to you than I can." She leaned forwards and pointed to the map, "See, here is the monastery. You will be there in no time at all." She opened the notepad and wrote the name of the Metro stop out for me. I read it out loud and she corrected my pronunciation. She jotted down directions to the monastery and it all seemed quite clear. "If Father M. is not there, one of the other fathers will take care of you."

From what she was saying it sounded as though I might make the trip only to find him unavailable. I wasn't keen. I stared at the map and nodded and pushed the objections out of my mind: once I had accepted the idea, all my anxiety left me and I thanked her for her help.

"This is our last chance to speak," she said, "is there anything specific you want to talk about? I do not have long this morning, so let's use the time we have."

"I've been thinking a lot about how people of your generation lived through persecution. Being here now, in such a beautiful city, with churches being built and the freedom to worship, it's hard to imagine that it really happened so recently. I have never been among Christians who were persecuted for their faith before. Is there something you can tell me about this?"

"Do you mean the actual experience? Do you want me to describe what they did to us?"

"No, I was wondering more about how you think of it. How you understand it in terms of your faith?"

"Perhaps how we wonder that God let this happen to us?" She said.

I nodded, unsure of how to answer. Her expression grew serious and she said, "When God permits afflictions to befall us it is an opportunity to learn patience. Without patience we cannot endure anything. God permitted the Russian people to become bearers of suffering so that we would be trained into real soldiers. The spiritual warfare needs front line troops, but you don't send children to the front line. We had many martyrs who came from among us, I knew a priest who was executed. He was a quiet man, there was nothing outwardly remarkable about him. One day the police came to arrest him and we never saw him again. God made us true soldiers in His army, and do you think the war is over? Our enemy continues to wage war against us, just as he has done from the beginning, but we have been taught how to fight him. When persecution comes, the Church learns that only by living according to God's commandments can we survive. I mean survive spiritually. These are lessons that cannot be learned in times of comfort and ease. The only road to salvation is the cross. God grants us afflictions that we may follow our Lord to Calvary. All afflictions are an opportunity to come closer to God, they break us, they soften our proud hearts. Only through being humbled by suffering do we begin to understand God's love, and realising how completely God loves us brings joy to our hearts even when the world sees only suffering."

Her eyes were glazed with the remembrance of things beyond my experience or understanding; I felt ashamed of the comfortable life I had always known. She smiled and said, "God knows all our hearts. He sees our weakness. We must never lose hope. There is an eternal reward awaiting every one of us, according to the degree to which we have laboured for God. When we understand this, we rejoice in the temptations of this world."

"In the West we know very little of this," I admitted.

"Thanks be to God for your freedoms. We must not long for persecution, when the savages take control there are all kinds of evils set loose. But in the West you have different trials, many of them as hard to bear as firing squads and labour camps. Many saints warned us that in the last days the faithful will be attacked by comfort and worldly treasures. The illusions of this world can deceive Christians into losing their minds. If we forget even for a day that we must die and answer for our lives, we start to live like the pagans. But all around the world people are afraid. This Coronavirus has caught people unready. There is panic at the thought of death, people feel cheated. Christians must set an example by accepting the cross God gives them. There is no greater medicine for the soul than physical illness, it brings us to our senses and calls us to a Christian way of life. We must be ready to endure without complaint anything that God permits to come upon us. What joy there is in our suffering when we know that our burdens will be our resurrection. This is the heart of the Russian people. We have carried a heavy cross for the sake of the whole world. Today we are seeing a time of blessing, and I pray that Christians everywhere will hear the voice of truth that still cries out while the voices of the world tell them lies. On your news programmes and in your newspapers Russia is criticised because it holds on to Christian values. Whose voice do you think is heard when they attack us for refusing to bow to the new philosophies of this age? It certainly is not the voice of God." She paused, and said, "These voices are very loud, and the voice of God is a gentle whisper. While men fill their ears with the cries of the world, they rebel and say God does not speak to them, that God does not answer their prayers. The more we listen to the world, the harder it is for us to hear God. But western culture is encouraging a universal spiritual deafness."

"What do you think is the most important lesson in all this?" I asked.

"I would say the remembrance of death," she said in a hushed voice. "Call to mind your death as often as you can. We can only defend our soul against the vanities of this world so long as we are aware of our death. When the Day of Judgement comes, how much of our life will shame us? What use have we made of the time God gave us? The accomplishments and honours of this world will all pass away, but the good deeds we have performed for our Lord will be eternal. The devil works night and day to convince us of how important this world is, but it's a lie. And the remembrance of death helps us to silence that lie. When we are lying in the darkness of the grave, our soul will cry out at the emptiness of everything this world has to offer. In the grave the vanity of our ambitions will be mocked, and we will know how foolish we have been."

"It is hard to defend ourselves against worldly thinking when we live in the world," I said. "We can't all live in a monastery."

Mother D. shook her head, "There have been many saints who had families and lived in cities. The external circumstances of our lives are not what constitutes the wilderness. There have been hermits whose hearts have been filled with earthly desires. And there are husbands and wives who have lived like angels. The pleasures and temptations we overcome are the battles God permits us to fight, where ever we are. He permits us temptations so that we can become true warriors and learn to fight. Unless we learn the art of spiritual warfare we will have no shield, or sword, or helmet."

"For many people," I said, "it is hard to know even where to begin."

"All of our hearts can be darkened by the things of this world. The pleasures and sensations that the body craves darken the heart. Our soul can be so darkened that it chooses the works of darkness. The reality of pain and the truth of suffering drive sensuality out of the heart. So you see, pain can make the heart ready to receive the Holy Spirit. The Comforter cannot comfort one who knows no pain. This is the source of our joy, when God's Holy Spirit transforms our suffering into victory, our Calvary becomes a resurrection."

"This is almost the exact opposite of what we are taught in the West," I said. "Christianity has become a way of finding some kind of assurance against the difficulties of life. The truth of Orthodoxy is alien to our culture."

"But not to men's hearts," Mother D. said gently. "The human heart is created with a mystery so deep that no culture or upbringing can penetrate to the depths of where it longs for God. Our children were taught by atheists in school, they were told that the priests and monks were lying to them to take their money. But look at us now, the hearts of the people still yearned for God. True theology is not learned through schools or universities, but by protecting our hearts from the world and being with God. Theology is born of prayer, and every human heart is made to pray. Even a small taste of the Kingdom of heaven can be enough to give us a thirst for God. A tiny spark can set the whole of our soul ablaze. The West is in a dangerous condition, but when God's fire catches, it can run rampant very quickly. The whole of Russia is on fire once more, you must pray that England will catch the flame."

Almost without pausing she glanced at her watch and said, "I must go now. Your blessing, Father."

Without any great farewell she kissed my hand, swilled the cups in the sink and bowed briefly before leaving. I followed her out of the little room and after turning and smiling, she quickly walked back to the enclosed area of the monastery. As the door swung shut behind her I knew our time together was over, and I thanked God for this extraordinary woman. I looked down at the sheet of paper she had given me and practiced the name of the station one more time. My heart had begun to settle on what she had told me to do. I venerated the icons in one of the side chapels and back on the street outside I decided to eat my lunch in Gorky Park.

Chapter Fifteen

Bolshoy Moskvoretsky Bridge had become my usual route to Red Square. On the near side of the river there is a small supermarket that sells fresh food and I had become a regular there. A tough-looking security guard who stood at the door had begun to carry my empty basket from the till and hold open the doors for me. Many of the pre-cooked vegetable dishes looked completely alien to me, and unable to read the contents I often took pot luck in what I was buying. I was trying hard to select fasting food, but when sitting on a bench in Gorky Park I discovered what looked like sliced fruit turned out to be thick cut chips. I knew they had been deep fried but I wasn't prepared to throw them away. They were delicious. With them I had a tray of pickled vegetables that were sufficiently unpleasant to relieve me of any guilt I might have felt about the chips. To accompany the food I had a bottle of carrot juice which proved to be the best part of the meal. I ate slowly, savouring what I could, the cold air pinching at my cheeks.

I sat looking out over the Moskva River, feeling very content. I tried to reflect on Mother D.'s words and it was as though I had been given a great treasure to take home with me. I was frustrated with how I had reacted to her suggestion of visiting the other monastery and it made me see the timidity that was affecting my choices. Travelling alone to Russia had felt such a confident thing to do, but I could see that in reality I was only confident because I felt in control of what was happening. Mother D.'s comments about our mortality reminded me of what an illusion it is to imagine we have control over our lives, and I knew I needed to trust more in God. It was hard to think about death in such a beautiful place, but as I looked at the Kremlin walls the memory of the martyrs shook away my contentment. I pushed my hand into my pocket and began to run the knots of my prayer rope through my fingers. The Jesus Prayer enabled me to become more sober and once I had completed the little rope I decided to take a walk further along the river.

Gorky Park was designed and brought into existence under the Communists in 1928. Prior to 2011 the park had been filled with amusement rides, but a major restoration transformed it into the elegant place it is today. What were deemed "illegal objects" were removed and new soil and gardens were laid. In that same year an enormous ice rink was installed that covers fifteen thousand square metres. As I walked along, cyclists sped by in their designated lanes and every now and then young men rode by on futuristic looking motorised wheels that were controlled by tilts of the body. Even on a Tuesday there were many families out walking together, and it was easy to see why the park is such a favourite place for Muscovites.

I continued on towards the Krymsky Bridge, a steel suspension design that leads to Crimean Square. Another remnant from Stalin's reign, the bridge was built in 1938, and despite the period from which it comes, is a stunning construction. Stalin had ordered that all Moscow bridges be destroyed and replaced with modern designs, as part of his plan to rejuvenate the city. The old wooden bridge that had originally spanned the river there had been the crossing point since 1786, and as I walked the six hundred plus metres across its arc I looked back down the river at the other bridge I had so often crossed.

I followed the main road, known as the Garden Ring and by-passed the impressive looking Moscow Museum. Eventually I reached signs pointing to The Ministry of Foreign Affairs, and as I studied my map I looked up to see a sign in English declaring the Hard Rock Café. As I read it I knew I had strayed too far into a different part of Moscow and wanting to avoid anything that would make me feel more of a tourist than I already did, I retreated back along the route I had come by.

At the bridge I was surprised at how long it had taken me to complete the walk and I decided to return to my room. I had begun to think about my plans for Wednesday and hoped that by sorting out my route to the airport I would feel more relaxed. Despite walking at a good pace the Moscow air kept me cool and by the time I reached the Pilgrim Centre I was tired but somehow energised.

In my room I took out my Kindle and began searching online maps for the closest Metro stations. There were a good number, but as I tried to figure out which line I needed my lack of Russian left me confused. I turned my attention to reaching Donskoy Monastery, and as Mother D. had said, it looked a straight journey through to Shabolovskaya from a nearby station. I had another go at my airport journey but again it was too complicated for me. A little frustrated I sent a message to A. and V. asking if they could take a look at the Metro time table and tell me which train to catch. By the time I had returned from the kitchen with a cup of tea A. had responded.

"Dear Father Spyridon, what time do you need to reach the airport?"

I told her my flight wasn't until ten to five in the morning, which meant catching the last Aeroexpress train before midnight. Like most international airports in capital cities around the world, Moscow has a train service that carries travellers from the underground system, but they don't run in the early hours of the morning. Within a few minutes A. responded again, "We will pick you up from your room at ten and travel with you on the Metro to the Aeroexpress." This would mean they would be travelling home at nearly midnight. I couldn't believe their kindness, and ordinarily I would have refused such an offer, but I was so relieved at knowing I would make it to the airport I tried to let them know how grateful I was to them once again. As I sipped at my tea I saw that it was nearly time for vespers. This was to be my last time worshipping with the community there, I had only one day left in Russia before the flight back to London. I pulled on my rassa and stepped out into the evening air; from within the church there was the sound of singing and I rushed to the door to join them.

Chapter Sixteen

Clutching my tourist map I followed the roads to the Metro. The stations are easy to spot as a large red letter 'M' hangs above each one, and there are two hundred and fourteen of them scattered across the city. The entrance was a series of wooden doors that looked like they belonged to an opera house rather than an underground station, and inside a glass chandelier completed the impression. Next to the ticket office were automatic machines, but I assumed I would have more luck with a living person than a computer. I joined the short queue and quickly found myself before a young woman in a smart uniform. I spoke the name of my destination, having practiced it all the way from my room, and in perfect English she asked if it was a single or return journey. With relief I told her I needed to get back and she informed me I could buy a tourist card for one or a number of days if I wanted to make several journeys. As this was my last day there was no reason to buy anything but the one ticket I needed, but I made a mental note of this for the future. After slipping my ticket through the window she told me to follow the coloured arrows and pointed to my right, and when I thanked her in Russian her smile suggested my accent needed some work.

I gazed up at a map of the Metro lines. The centre of the city has a huge circular line from which smaller lines run out creating the appearance of a spider's web. I knew which colour and number to look for, and without this I would have been lost. But it turned out to be much simpler than I had imagined, and following the line back to my station I decided I needed platform three. I waved my card over an automated reader and the turn-style opened before me. The flow of passengers led me forward to the escalator, a long white tunnel that carried us deep underground. Even here the lighting came from large globes on metal pillars that looked artistic and elegant. Once at the bottom there were signs in Cyrillic lettering pointing in different directions, but they all had the colour codes and numbers which were easy to follow.

The tunnels were arched stone decorated with carvings of flowers, and the walls were adorned with classical Russian paintings. On the floor were stickers that repeated the information from the signs, as well as the names of the stops. I pulled out a slip of paper to confirm the name I was reading was the one Mother D. had written, and my confidence continued to grow as I happily saw that they matched.

The tunnel opened out into a broad pair of platforms, with the name of the station on gold lettering on the walls. Next to the station name was a list of the stops and the direction of the train that the platforms served, and I joined the handful of people waiting at my platform. Thankfully I didn't have to deal with transferring to another train, it was a straight run and it was simply a matter of counting the passing stations until I reached Shabolovskaya.

After less than a minute the lights of the approaching train appeared in the darkness of the tunnel and the carriages pulled up alongside us. Russian Metro trains have a less rounded design than those in the West, and as the doors opened it was exciting to be in an environment so different to home. There were plenty of seats and I sat as near to the doors as I could in case I miscalculated the stops and needed to get out quickly. Above the windows were advertisements that looked very old-fashioned, with lots of pictures of smiling girls and bright colours. It was clear that the advertising business in Russia had not yet adopted the levels of manipulation we have become accustomed to in England.

The train pulled away. Around me sat a mixture of young people staring into mobile 'phones and older people reading newspapers or just staring ahead in the way that underground passengers do all over the world to avoid eye contact with anyone. I had been warned that some parts of the Metro are inhabited by stray dogs who curl up and sleep on the seats, but to my disappointment there were none to be seen. The same Russian friend had given me a tip which proved to be true. On Metro trains, the announcer is always male on journeys into the centre of Moscow, and as you cross the centre of the city and begin to head out the voice switches to female. As we approached our first stop I was reassured to hear the announcer was a woman who spoke in both Russian and English. This system of male and female voices was created to assist blind people, but it is also of benefit to uncertain Englishmen.

As the platforms at Shabolovskaya appeared alongside the carriage I stood gripping the bar above my head, eager to set out for the monastery. The doors opened to a place very different to the stations I had seen before. Though it had been built along with the rest of the Kaluzhskaya Line in 1962, there were problems with the long escalator shaft that meant the station remained closed for eighteen years. During this time the builders modernised its design, adding a stained-glass window celebrating various media personalities, and the walls were changed to white marble. As I walked the length of the platform I thought at first that the window was a religious image, and it was only as I drew closer that I realised that the Communists had appropriated the style for a secular purpose. The white walls and series of small archways would have turned any other building a target for sight-seers, and it was hard to believe so much care had been devoted to an underground station.

Outside the station the road was busy with traffic. The Metro is located next to a tram and bus station, and despite the lines of trees it felt very urban. The Metro station itself is a very low, flat roofed building that gives no hint of what lies beneath. I checked my map and it gave the impression that the monastery was very close. I took my bearings from a large four-storey building and hoped that even if I was on the wrong road my destination would be easy to spot. A few minutes later I was proved right, five dark blue onion domes, arranged in the traditional style of four around the central dome, stood out above the surrounding buildings. As I got closer I began to realise what a large complex of buildings it is. A high red wall protected the perimeter of its grounds, and its towers gave the impression of an army fortress. In fact its military appearance is no accident, it was founded in 1591 to commemorate Russia's victory over an invading Crimean army. But even further back than this, the monastery marks the site where Dimitry Domskoy had placed the icon of Our Lady of the Don after taking it into battle against the Tatars in 1380: the enemy fled without a fight. By the eighteenth century the monastery was in possession of many windmills, fisheries, and thousands of peasants. But the Soviets closed it down and it was here that Patriarch Tikhon was held after his arrest. In their usual fashion the Communists tried to remove the religious character of the place by turning it into an orphanage and a storage facility, but this human philosophy passed away and from 1992 the glory of God has been proclaimed there once more.

As I walked through the large entrance gates I wasn't sure where to go. The church was the obvious choice and as I approached it I gazed up at the three storey-structure that supported the towers and domes. There was a gentleness to the soft pink of the walls that made the impressive building look welcoming. I turned the handle of the old wooden door and wasn't prepared for the astonishing beauty of its interior. The walls were white and gold, the sense of space and light was incredible, but this was as nothing compared to the iconostasis. At its centre was an icon of the Virgin of the Don, and stretching high above it were eight tiers of icons which it was impossible to take in all at once, which were carved in the seventeenth century.

For a moment I had forgotten why I had come, so absorbed was I in the beauty of the church. I turned and stared at the high, intensely coloured frescoes, and only then did I see a man sitting beside the entrance. He nodded as I went up to him but when I asked for Father M. he shook his head and spoke quickly in Russian. I repeated Father M.'s name and there was a look of recognition in his face. He raised his finger to tell me to wait and pulled out a large mobile 'phone from under his desk. I couldn't follow what he was saying, but he lowered the 'phone and nodded repeating Father M.'s name. He said he would be there in five minutes and I thanked him for his help.

I was standing in front of the iconostasis when Father M. approached me. He looked to be in his early sixties, of average height, with a short grey beard and long hair tied back and tucked inside the collar of his rassa. At his chest glinted the Saint Nicholas pectoral cross worn by all Russian priests (on the instruction of Tsar Nicholas in order to distinguish them from deacons). We bowed and greeted each other with a kiss, "Welcome to the monastery, Father," he said with a strong accent.

"Thank you, I had no idea it was so big."

He nodded, "It has a curious history, some people have been scandalised by it. The Freemasons had a hand in some of the design, the domes above us point to the four points on the earth, and they managed to get a few symbols placed here and there. But of course, we will have nothing to do with them today, and their influence has been removed. But some people still feel sensitive about it." He laughed to himself, "The demons have been driven out, and the doors have been closed to any of their kind of influence." As he spoke deep lines creased around his eyes, suggesting he had laughed many times before. "Would you like to venerate Saint Tikhon before we talk?"

He led me out past some graves, "We have many artists, philosophers and members of aristocratic families buried here. I am sure that being close to so many prayers has helped them reach Heaven."

As we turned a corner I was surprised to see two tanks guarding the path. "They are a sign of our past," he said, "Russians do not forget what it has taken to get us where we are today. During the war with the Nazis, many abbots told their monks to enlist and fight for their homeland. The defence of our nation has been God's will. If Russia falls, how will the world know the truth about Christ?"

The second church had a familiar golden dome that did look like a flame burning in the sky. Father

M. crossed himself as he led me in and took me to the holy saint's relics. I kissed the icon above the reliquary and Father M. said "Our holy Patriarch endured for his people. When the Communists were faced with a famine in 1922 they accused the patriarch of many trumped up charges, and locked him away here saying he was a saboteur. They forged documents saying he had declared his support for them, but no one believed they were real. Eventually the fake church structure that the Communists created deposed him, but Orthodoxy has always maintained him as a Patriarch. Do you see, Father, how worldly powers can mimic the Church in order to deceive the faithful? But the Holy Spirit guides His people, this is how it will be until the final day."

As we walked out of the Church Father M. grew quiet as he reflected on what he had said. As we stepped into the cold sunshine he continued, "The faithful people of God will be attacked with all kinds of lies. They will be told to accept union with Rome, with schismatics, with Protestants and even non-Christian faiths. There will be bishops who abandon the faith, and there will be those who stay true to the Church. But there will always be faithful people who refuse to follow heretics. The people recognise a true bishop when God sends them one. The Orthodoxy of a bishop is felt in everything he does, not just his words, but his love of truth, his defence of tradition, and the people see this for what it is. I have great confidence in our ordinary laity, thanks be to God for their simple faith." He seemed to catch himself saying these things, and almost apologetically he said, "I do not wish to appear to be criticising our bishops. Imagine how hard the demons work to make them fall. We priests and monks know how intense the spiritual battle becomes when we are ordained. Think how the demons would rejoice at causing a bishop to fall. We must all pray for them."

He took me to a building near the outer wall where he invited me to sit at a table in a plain office that could have been a room in any building in the world except for the small icon of the Mother of God that hung on the far wall. Next to us a large portrait of Patriarch Kyrill hung in a golden frame. There was no kettle; his intention was clearly to talk and nothing else. He asked me about Orthodoxy in the United Kingdom, and listened carefully to what I had to say. When I had finished describing my parish I said, "Father, you talked about how the faithful could be deceived. How are they to know who to believe?"

"This is simple," he said, "as long as they know the faith and tradition of the Church, anything alien to it will have a bad smell. But in the end, only prayer protects us from lies."

"I'm not sure I understand what you mean by this," I admitted.

"If our people pray, God will be close to them, and they will recognise anything that comes from Satan. This is how it has always been. If we live our faith, it means we are spiritual beings, we live for Heaven; the lies of this world do not match our experience of God. Even when those lies are dressed up with half-truths and Christian sounding words. They will tell the people to accept things in the name of unity or love, but the unity of the Church comes from Christ, it cannot be manufactured by men. Unless we share the one faith, the truth, then what kind of unity are we talking about? Worldly unity insists that Orthodox people stop being so strict about their faith, perhaps let a few things fall away in order to get on with people. We will be told to stop being so unreasonable, and in the end the world will paint us as the evil ones because we do not go along with antichrist's plans for a global identity. They will create all kinds of global catastrophes that need the world to act as one, but make no mistake, we know exactly where this is all leading."

He watched me carefully and for a moment our eyes locked. When he was satisfied that I had understood his point he said, "We must guard the spirit of Orthodoxy, because without it even the words of great saints will lose their meaning to us. This is true of all Christian texts, even the gospels. We must nurture the spiritual interpretation of what is written, there is so much symbolism that we cannot see with a worldly mind. It is the language of the spirit that deals with the inner experience of Christian life, and we can only begin to understand it when we have purified our hearts. This is why I say prayer protects us from lies. We must repent of our sins, follow Christ's commandments, and only then do we begin to understand greater depths of truth, because Christ is the Truth, and true understanding is found in Him. When we live closer to Him, we are illuminated by His truth. It is not something we can describe in worldly language, it is beyond the material things we see and experience, and material language is inadequate to describe it. Of course, purity of heart is overcoming the passions, and unless we clean ourselves of them we cannot draw closer to what is holy and pure."

I nodded as I followed his words, "And the passions infect us in so many ways," I said.

"Yes, the passions are a spiritual infection that sickens the soul. In the West you have such high rates of depression, this is a consequence of the passions."

"But there is growing depression in Russia too," I insisted.

"Oh yes, and alcoholism too," he said. "You see, when we awake the passions but are unable to satisfy their demands, we become angry or fall into depression. Modern man tries to explain depression with all kinds of psychological excuses, but the reality is that when we are depressed it is because we have fallen prey to the passions. And more than this, the passions dull the heart so that we lose our sensitivity to God's grace. We can no longer sense what God is doing with us, we fail to see how His compassion and love is working in our lives. Instead we grow resentful: only when we see that our anger is never justified can we begin to deal with it."

"How do we even begin to repent of them when they have such a grip on us?" I said.

"The first step in overcoming anger is not to express it. Our Lord said we must turn the other cheek. He was not just talking about when someone slaps us, but was telling us how to change our hearts. We must forgive inwardly, let go of our anger. This is how we attain purity in the heart: by being purified of the passions. Our Lord instructed us to be pure of heart, and so long as we allow anger and depression to live in us there is no purity."

"I understand," I said, "but is there anything practical we can do to achieve this."

"Beyond prayer we can turn the passions around and make them the means of repentance. When we are self-reflective, when we look closely at ourselves, we can identify their presence in us and use them to prompt us to change. Anger can indicate that passions are at work in us, and we have to follow the path from which anger has come to find which passions are there. Anger can be like a flag that waves and lets us know about passions we might not be aware of."

"This is the spiritual understanding you were talking about?" I said.

"Partly, yes. But I am a modern man, I too have lost the way of thinking that existed in the early Church. The Apostles understood Christ's teaching more fully than us, they saw the spiritual truth. They taught this to those around them, and in the writings of the Church Fathers we are able to glimpse this truth even today. The gospels are the richest statements to be found on earth, but too often we skim over the surface of their meaning. The events, the words Christ spoke, it is God speaking to the world, it speaks to the soul, offers us the way of transformation. The gospels are filled with spiritual power. When grace is at work in us we begin to learn from the gospels, but it is a knowledge that the world cannot teach. In fact I would say that when we think and understand in a worldly way it is then that we can fall into despair."

"The modern world is full of traps," I said.

"The devil is cunning. We must simplify our lives, let go of conveniences and the desire for comfortable homes and their worldly riches. Desire for any of this brings us misery. Think of the saints who gave everything they had to the poor in order to follow Christ. We must turn our backs on the vanities of this world because there is a banquet prepared for us in Heaven." He smiled and said, "Some have even begun to taste it in this life."

He looked away for a moment and as I followed his gaze I saw two birds perched in the tree outside the window. Father M. turned back to me and said, "The world will call us crazy, and if we are truly Christian, from the world's view we are crazy. We have nothing in common with the pursuits of this world, we are strangers here; we belong to another place. It is this reality that must guide us so that we aren't fooled by those traps and deceits that the devil has filled this world with."

Once more he paused and his face grew a little pensive as he followed his thoughts. His eyes focussed on the table in front of him and I wondered if he was going to say anything more. But he looked up at me and said, "The root of much of this is the way we think about death. The world has truly misunderstood what it means. The truth is we should fear sin more than we fear death. Do we not believe it will be better to be with God than to live in this world? Where is the joy that such hope brings? We should feel more joy over the next life than for anything in this world. Death is not to be feared. The devil doesn't want us to think like this. He wants us afraid, and he wants the way we live and all our choices based in fear. This is how we lose hope and fall into anxiety."

"What is the best weapon against this?" I asked.

"All our hope must stem from Christ's promise that if we repent, He will accept us. This is the power of repentance. We must remember, even the demons, if they repented, God would forgive them. Think of that! The demons who have chosen evil for thousands of years, who have brought so much misery and suffering to mankind: even they would receive mercy from God if they repented. But they refuse. Their hatred of God, and of us because they see His image in us, is so consuming that they choose evil even in the face of God's Judgement. Perhaps we can see why a being that has been so corrupted would reject God's love, but a man? We are created in God's image, the divine image is within us; we were created to be sons of God, how terrifying it is that so many men should turn away from Him. To reject God when it is our nature to worship Him is worse than madness. And every one of us is capable of falling into this madness. Every time we choose sin, we reject God. Every time we sin we nail Christ to the cross and we embrace death. Such madness! Such ingratitude!" Father M. began to lightly tap the tip of his finger on the table to emphasise his words. "Can we be surprised that there is such depression in the world when we choose to live in hell? Because make no mistake, these poor souls are already tasting separation from God. When we choose to alienate ourselves from God, of course we despair. And no matter how hard we chase the rewards and pleasures of this world, we can never find peace. In fact, the harder we run after material comfort, the further we run from God."

"But if people are fooled into doing this," I said, "can they really be held responsible?"

"In some ways, of course, there are times when the demons lay their traps and we are caught unawares; but this is not the whole story. God abandons no one. Even the man who has fallen for the trickery of temptation, he will have a moment when his eyes open and he knows he has a choice. God has given us free will, we are never completely without responsibility. How could anyone be judged by God if they did not choose good or evil? We cannot make excuses for ourselves, even men who live their whole lives in the jungle, God reaches them. There will have been an opportunity in their heart to respond to God. But we who have heard the Gospel, what excuse can we make? So let us repent quickly, before it is too late. Let us hear God's prompting of our hearts. Time is slipping away."

He quietly sighed and I sensed a great weight of concern was pressing down on him, a burden of love for people everywhere. His compassion made it easy to open my heart to him and I said, "Is there anything you can say that will help me protect myself when I return to England? Materialism is pushed much more there, it is a constant battle to refuse it."

"The Fathers have given us plenty of advice," he said. "They remind us that those who store up earthly treasures attract thieves who come to rob them. They grow suspicious, their heart is where their treasure is: locked away in a dark vault. But when we fill our heart with heavenly treasures, they overflow and people around us may grow rich too. God's love lightens the darkest rooms. When we are filled with this light we even see into the dark corners of our own souls. It is painful to recognise the sin within us, what else can we do when we see it but mourn, shed tears and entreat God's forgiveness. But our mourning is filled with an unearthly joy, because our hope is in God's love for us. Without such hope we could not repent and we would join the world in its despair. But when we taste God's love, such misery is impossible. Even in the face of death, the martyrs rejoiced because their hope was not found in anything of this world. But equally, the man whose heart trusts in earthly consolations will despair in the end. It is inevitable."

Father M. looked at me and smiled, "Will you join us for lunch, Father? It is not very much, but you are welcome."

I looked at my watch, "Thank you, but I need to head back. I'm flying home tonight and I need to finish packing."

He smiled, "Thank you for visiting, it has been good to meet you. I pray you have a safe flight."

We stood and he gestured for me to go ahead of him. He walked me to the monastery gate pointing out different buildings and monuments. As we parted I felt a longing to remain with him, he communicated a deep peace that it was impossible to be unaffected by. He held my hands in his and squeezed them tightly, "God is with you," he whispered. He turned and walked back along the footpath, his prayer rope running through his fingers.

The route back to the Metro was fairly straightforward, I glanced at my map a few times but eventually I could see the blue M above the station and I crossed through the traffic. All thoughts of the airport were gone, I found myself immersed in Father M.'s words and I felt a strong compulsion to pray. I waved my travel card over the scanner and descended on the escalator back down into the depths of the Metro system. I paid little attention to the decoration around me, and within thirty seconds of being on the platform the train pulled alongside us. There were no available seats and I stood near the doorway, holding onto a bar that ran from the floor to the ceiling. The train lurched forwards and I checked a piece of paper from my pocket to confirm how many stops I should count before leaving the train. We reached the first station within a few minutes and many of the passengers vacated the carriage, leaving lots of empty seats. As I sat down I studied the map on the carriage wall that showed where we were heading. I didn't recognise any of the names, and it quickly dawned on me that I was on the wrong train. I tried to stay calm and decided to get off at the next station and go back to my starting point. One of the good things about the Moscow Metro is there is rarely a wait of more than a minute or two between trains, and I told myself there wasn't going to be a problem.

As I waited on the platform of a station whose name I couldn't read, I stared at the map of the train lines on the wall opposite, and with relief recognised Shabolovskaya. The next train arrived and I rode it back down towards where I had just come from. It was a huge relief to eventually be back at the station I knew and I went down the tunnel to the base of the escalator. I realised I had mistaken the names of two stations which appeared similar, and satisfied that I was heading in the right direction I found the right platform. When I was in the carriage I double-checked the map above my head and knew I was on the right train. The return journey seemed to take less time than the outward ride and soon I was back on the street following my map to the Pilgrim Centre.

The brevity of my life was tangible and even the solid buildings around me had taken on an appearance of being temporary. The concrete and steel structures were flimsy in the face of eternity, and I sensed the passing of time. As I walked I tried to take in as much as I could, knowing that this time tomorrow, God willing, I would be home. The realisation brought images of my wife and sons and strangely, now that I was so close to seeing them, I found myself missing them more than at any other time in my trip.

Chapter Seventeen

Back in my room I checked for messages from home and sent a reminder of when I would be arriving at Heathrow. There was a message from A. and V. to let me know they would be coming a little earlier than necessary. I was relieved, after the mix up that had caused them to be late the previous night and I didn't want to risk anything going wrong when there was an aeroplane to catch.

I checked the time, it was twenty to six; nearly time for vespers in the church. I had assumed I wouldn't be able to worship with them again but the opportunity was too good to miss. It would leave me a few hours to gather my things and clean up before setting off. As usual the church was full and the choir sang as beautifully as ever. The hour and a half passed quickly and I hoped the busy night ahead wouldn't completely strip me of the prayerful attitude. The service was led by a priest I didn't know and afterwards I slipped away unnoticed. In the room I sat at my desk and made a few notes about the day. Father M.'s words were still affecting me and I spent some time alone in prayer. I tried to read a little but found it hard to concentrate and kept glancing at my watch. In the end, other than tidying the room, I achieved very little during my final few hours alone, and my growing sense of excitement over the journey left me with little peace.

At ten to ten I received a message to tell me A. and V. would be with me in five minutes. I made one last check to be sure I hadn't left anything behind and went out to return my keys. The church and office were both locked and I wasn't sure what to do, but as I stood wondering a young woman who I recognised from the choir came round the corner. I explained my problem and she kindly made a call for me. "He will be here in a few minutes," she said. As she walked away A. and V. appeared in the darkness and we exchanged greetings. We waited for barely a minute when one of the men who worked for the Pilgrim Centre came to collect my key. He spoke no English and I felt I hadn't adequately expressed how grateful I was as he disappeared again.

"The Metro isn't far," V. said. He offered to carry my bag but as I only had the one I refused. The night air was particularly cold and it was the first time in the whole trip that I needed the heavy overcoat I had brought with me after being advised to do so by my Russian friends in England; I was looking forward to telling them how mild it had been.

"What time will you get home?" I asked, aware that A. and V. had made a special trip out to help me.

"That doesn't matter," V. said, waving his hand. "We are happy to help." I pushed him on it but he wouldn't be drawn to give an answer.

188

The Metro was about ten minutes' walk away and in the night the sign glowed brightly above the street. They insisted on using their travel card to pay for my entry and once again we were descending on a steep escalator. There were very few people around at this time of night and there was a surreal feeling moving through the network of tunnels that were so quiet. I would have had difficulty finding the right platform without them, and as usual we waited barely a couple of minutes before the train arrived. We chatted very little on the ride, but my Russian guides exchanged regular smiles with me to confirm they were happy to be of help. Their kind demeanour only reinforced the opinion I had of them.

The underground took us to a larger station where the Aeroexpress trains are caught. I had chosen Domodedovo Airport over Sheremetyevo because I had read online that the transport links make it easier to get to. But in reality, the Aeroexpress shuttle serves both just as well, and I could have made the choice more on geography than the misleading information on the internet. The station was a long building, and almost everything was shut. At the far end we could see guards and an open kiosk, and we headed that way. A. started talking to the guards in Russian, and despite my limited knowledge of the language, I could tell from the way they were pointing back up to the other end of the station that we were in the wrong place. We retraced our steps and found the ticket office. Again A. asked for the ticket and I slipped the cash over the counter. The woman serving us explained where we should catch the train and we followed her directions. The platform was closed until twenty minutes before the train was to depart, and a small queue of travellers heading for the airport had started to form. I thanked A. and V. for all their help, and realising I was anticipating that they would leave V. said "No, Father, we will wait until your train leaves."

"But you will be so late getting home," I said.

"Please," he insisted, "we are happy to wait."

I laid my bags down and said "I have had a good trip. I didn't expect Moscow to be so beautiful."

"It is a good city, but like anywhere else it has its problems. I feel that our government is too concerned with international politics rather than the situation here at home."

"I think your president is forced into this with such an aggressive US regime. Russia is surrounded by NATO military bases," I said.

"Of course, we understand this, and we are grateful that we have a strong president. After the fall of the Soviets, many of us, me included, welcomed the changes that came to Russia. We saw the economic benefits that western people enjoyed and we believed we would share that lifestyle. It is true that capitalism has brought benefits, but the social changes that this introduced do not fit with Russian attitudes. Some people have been allowed to become very rich, but most people struggle. I do not think most Russians trust

America, and capitalism is still associated with it, it is hard for us to separate the two in our minds."

"Is that a result of the cold war years?" I asked.

"For many older people there may be truth in this, we heard nothing but anti-western propaganda from the media. But amongst young people this feeling is just as strong. Russians understand the value in their traditions, they want to protect what they have from a culture that has abandoned Christianity. This is partly why President Putin is so popular, he stands up for Christian values, and the more he pushes against western liberalism, the more the people support him. We have only recently emerged from a time when the Church was attacked, people are rushing back to their faith. But they do not forget so easily how savage the atheists were. Western culture is built on this atheism, and so many people are wary of trusting it too far."

"What do you think helped the Russian Church survive that time?"

"We have a long history of living the Orthodox faith. Families visited monasteries, holy shrines, the local church was at the heart of life. So when persecution came, we were ready." He turned to me with a grave expression and said, "When a culture has only Disneyland and fun parks to occupy them, they will not be ready for what is to come. And make no mistake, it can happen overnight. Suddenly rules change, laws are passed. Suddenly churches are closed and the struggle begins. But we have to be ready for it, we cannot face such evil unprepared."

V. spoke openly and at a volume that caused a few of the other people in the queue to look his way as he expressed himself. But there was no reaction, no one objected. I wanted to ask more, but one of the guards opened the gateway and we were allowed onto the platform. A modern looking train painted in the brightest red, sat waiting with its doors open. I was unsure whether to board or continue talking to A. and V. as there was still fifteen minutes or more before it was due to depart. But V. waved me forwards, "Please," he said, "you must take your seat."

I thanked them again for their kindness and they received a blessing. I stepped up into the train and walked to the middle of the carriage. V. and A. moved along the platform to stand outside my window, and I felt uncomfortable sitting in the warm comfort of the train while they shivered out on the platform. They looked small and vulnerable standing alone in the empty station and it was a relief when the alarm sounded and the doors slid shut. They waved and nodded, and only when the train was actually pulling away did they finally start their long journey home.

An electronic screen flickered into life and confirmation of our destination was announced in Russian and English. It was followed by a cartoon warning of the dangers of unattended bags. Unlike on the London underground where passengers are forced to listen to a children's nursery rhyme, "See it, say it, sort it", the Russian equivalent showed a bag full of dynamite. Such an image would be unheard of on any U.K. transport system, for fear that people would be too upset and complain. I admired the straightforwardness of the Russian outlook; even in a cartoon it was treating people like adults.

The journey to the airport took about thirty minutes, and I watched the lights of Moscow flashing by. The Aeroexpress station is a short walk to the airport entrance, and once inside I recognised the familiar balconies from eight days before. I found the British Airways counter in order to print off my boarding pass, but was told it wouldn't be open for another five hours. I still had plenty of roubles in my pocket and decided to treat myself to a good meal. On the floor above was a series of restaurants, all open but almost entirely empty of customers. I opted for one that looked like it had a good range of vegetarian dishes and as I moved my way along the counter selecting my meal I spotted shrimps. It was just as well that I had plenty of money left as the meal wasn't cheap, but the utter luxury of sitting eating shrimp while the Italian football league was broadcast on huge screens made the price worth paying. I replenished my coffee a couple of times and spent about three hours watching the games. The staff had no impulse to move me on, and it was unlike any other experience I had had all week. I was tired and a little anxious about the long flight, and instead of prayer I turned to soccer.

Eventually I decided to visit the chapel and found the same two women in attendance as a week before. One of them recognised me and gave me two magazines full of colour pictures of various Church hierarchs. I lit some candles and prayed for a safe flight, and being aware of standing before the same icon I had prayed before eight days earlier, I thanked God for the people I had met.

I took a look at the stalls which were still manned at four in the morning, and bought a few gifts for my family. From the balcony I could see people in British Airways uniform opening their gate and I went down to sign in. The woman who served me looked tired and I wondered if I looked the same to her. She gave me my pass and told me where to enter security. After eight days away from the BBC coverage of the Coronavirus I was surprised to see Russian staff wearing medical masks. The same scrutiny was applied to my documents as had been given to them on my entry into Russia, and though I had nothing to worry about, it was that same sense of relief when my passport was handed back to me. There were about a dozen travellers in total waiting to pass through security, and within five minutes I was wandering through duty free. I still had roubles I didn't want to take home, and fed machines for bottled water which I pushed into my bag.

There was an hour and a half wait before boarding, and tiredness was just beginning to take hold of me. I sat in a plastic chair, alternating between my book and my prayer rope, but with little success with either. Around me other travellers were sprawled out either sleeping or trying to sleep, but my mind was too busy to rest. Finally we were invited to board the aeroplane, and with less than thirty passengers we were told to sit where ever we wanted. After the usual safety instructions the aeroplane taxied its way round the various paths until we sat at the end of the runway. I took one last look at the Lettering spelling out "Moscow" on the front of the building, and the pilot hit the thrusters that launched us forwards.

Chapter Eighteen

The screen on the back of the seat in front of me offered a long list of choices for viewing during the flight. I hadn't seen a news broadcast for eight days and chose the BBC headlines. There was only one story: Coronavirus. In one week the few cases being reported in the U.K. had become the media obsession, and having missed the build-up I couldn't believe the hysteria I was seeing. After a few minutes I had had enough of it and switched to the map that plotted the aircraft's progress. It was exciting to read the names of the countries passing beneath us in the dark, and I imagined the people living amongst the little dots of light.

I tried to sleep but couldn't, and as I visited the toilet I was a little envious of the other passengers who were stretched out across the seats under their British Airways blankets. I chatted with one of the stewardesses in a hushed voice, and the whole scene was unlike any flight I had made before.

After a couple of hours I watched the sun rising from the darkness over the horizon. The sight of the red light emerge across the sky kept me transfixed, and I was aware of what a relatively new experience it was for human beings to witness it from such a height. As the map told us we were crossing the North Sea and heading towards the South-east of England the sky had turned a clear blue with a thick carpet of white clouds hiding the world from us. When the pilot announced that we would be landing in approximately twenty minutes the little icon of the aeroplane on the map changed course and circled back on itself. In our physical reality the aeroplane banked sharply and above us through the window I saw two other aeroplanes which looked to be flying far too close to each other and to us. Once back on our original course I could see four aeroplanes making the same loop and it was obvious Heathrow was too congested to let us in. We went on to circle three more times, making the same steep turns as before, and I had to overcome frustration over being so close to home but held back this way. It was an odd sensation being on such a large aeroplane as it made such manoeuvres. On the final loop the computerised icon of our aeroplane continued on and we were back on course and could feel ourselves beginning to descend.

The green fields of England were beautiful from above, and I felt a strong sense of connection with the land that wasn't something I would have anticipated; I knew this was home. We passed over the motorways that feed London and the buildings and cars continued to come closer as our altitude decreased. By the time we were approaching Heathrow we were barely a few metres from the ground and the true sense of our speed became apparent. The runway rose to meet us and with the familiar bump we were down.

I grabbed my bag and headed to the front of the aeroplane where the cabin crew performed their ritual thanks and farewell. The small group of us followed the signs that announced the departure terminals and even at the exits there were very few people around. Though the flight had taken three and a half hours, the time difference between Russia and the U.K. meant it was now only an hour after we had taken off. But despite the time gain on the clocks, my body was now struggling with its lack of sleep.

I found the train connection and within half an hour was back at Euston Underground Station which is just a short walk from Euston Station itself. The morning rush hour was now in full flow and there were many people wearing face masks. I had three hours to kill at Euston and went up to the restaurants on the balcony to drink as much coffee as I could to avoid nodding off. At one point a song by Ryan Adams played through the sound system and I smiled with recognition. The time dragged slowly, and with an hour still to go I walked down to the information boards. The area was packed, people were squeezed tightly up against each other and the board informed us that every train was delayed. The announcer kept telling everyone to remain in front of the boards to await instructions, and as time went on even more people joined the crowd. At one point a policeman led a very sick man through the middle of everyone. He was sweating and coughing; the very symptoms the BBC had been warning were signs of Covid 19. As he brushed past the waiting rail passengers there were murmurs of complaint but the policeman continued on regardless. This was the first time I had heard someone use the term "social distancing", and whatever the rail company had in mind, these were perfect conditions for ensuring the spread of the virus.

After another forty minutes the notice board switched from announcing delays to telling us that every train leaving Euston was cancelled. The reaction from the crowd was loud and angry, and there was a lot of confusion over what to do next. I went over to a man in rail uniform and asked his advice. He suggested I get on the underground and find another station to catch a train from. Not knowing London at all I asked which I should go to, and he told me to get to waterloo; but he couldn't guarantee that the different rail company would accept my ticket.

I lifted my bag back to my shoulder and weaved my way through the mass of people to an exit. I had wasted three hours waiting for a train that wasn't operating: if they had told us earlier I could have already been home. At the Underground Station I found myself amongst a number of people making the same attempt to catch another train and the ticket gate was opened to allow us through without tickets. We arrived at a very busy Waterloo Station and were told the train heading up to Birmingham was leaving in five minutes. Everyone rushed to the platform and the three little carriages were filled beyond capacity. People stood in every available space and it was clear that the conductor was not going to be able to get through to check our tickets. This was reassuring, and there was a great sense of relief when the train pulled away on time.

The unusual circumstances broke down the normal reserve amongst English train passengers, and there was a lot of sharing of complaints about how we had been treated. Some people were visibly upset at the experience, but most just simmered with anger. Most of us had no idea how to catch a train to Birmingham New Street from where we were heading and an old man loudly announced he knew the way and that we should all follow him. This is exactly what we did, and the young man at the ticket barrier waved us all through when a few people began to aggressively tell him what had happened. It was another thirty minute wait on the platform, but with so little of the journey left to make I was feeling content.

On the last train ride I called a local taxi service to pick me up at Telford, and I was assured there would be a car waiting for me. I kept a fifteen year old mobile 'phone just for these kinds of situations. At Telford Central I spotted my taxi and tapped on the window to ask the Asian driver to unlock the door. Seeing me dressed in black with a cross around my neck he shook his head and waved his hand in a gesture intended to move me away. I immediately rang the taxi firm again and as I did so the taxi drove away empty. The woman on the other end of the line said the driver was claiming his passenger hadn't shown up, and when I told her he had refused to let me in she insisted I was mistaken. As most of the taxis were now doing the school runs it was going to be thirty minutes before one could be sent out to me. I didn't have another taxi firm's telephone number and had to accept the wait. It was an odd feeling to have been treated this way for being dressed as a priest, and I was disappointed that it should happen in my own country. After so many stories about taxis in Russia, it was also ironic that this should be my experience in Britain. The second driver eventually showed up and for the whole ride shared his theories about the Coronavirus. His head was filled with all kinds of plots and conspiracies, and I realised how deeply the illness had entered people's consciousness. What I didn't know at this point was that if I had waited another two weeks to make my trip I wouldn't have been able to leave the country.

It was an odd scenario to come back to, and I had a profound sense of being far away from Moscow. Not just geographically, but culturally and socially; the British people understood the world in a completely different way. As the taxi made its way through the streets where my church community was based, I knew there was something of Holy Russia that we had to cling to if we were to survive everything that is to come. Now more than ever, we in the West must protect ourselves from the philosophies of our time, because despite the sweetness of its promises, I knew how dangerous the world around us had become.

9 781839 453670